Teaching Literacy

Engaging the Imagination of New Readers and Writers

To Mary, with best wishes, Kieran

Kieran Egan

CORWIN PRESS
A SAGE Publications Company
Thousand Oaks, California

Grateful acknowledgment is made to the American Association for the Advancement of Science (AAAS) for permission to reprint lessons from www.sciencenetlinks.com in Chapter 11.

For information:

Corwin Press
A Sage Publications Company
2455 Teller Road
Thousand Oaks, California 91320
www.corwinpress.com

Sage Publications Ltd.
1 Oliver's Yard
55 City Road
London EC1Y 1SP
United Kingdom

Sage Publications India Pvt. Ltd.
B-42, Panchsheel Enclave
Post Box 4109
New Delhi 110 017 India

Printed in the United States of America

Library of Congress Cataloging-in-Publication Data

Egan, Kieran.
Teaching literacy : engaging the imagination of new readers and writers / Kieran Egan.
    p. cm.
Includes bibliographical references and index.
ISBN 1-4129-2787-0 (cloth)—ISBN 1-4129-2788-9 (pbk.)
    1. Language arts (Elementary) I. Title.
LB1576.E336 2006
372.6—dc22   2005036542

This book is printed on acid-free paper.

06   07   08   09   10   9   8   7   6   5   4   3   2   1

Acquisitions Editor:	Stacy Wagner
Production Editor:	Laureen A. Shea
Copy Editor:	Marilyn Power Scott
Typesetter:	C&M Digitals (P) Ltd.
Proofreader:	Annette Pagliaro
Indexer:	Pamela Van Huss
Cover Designer:	Anthony Paular

Contents

Preface

This short book is intended to be both an advocate for and a guide to a new approach to teaching literacy. What is new about the approach is tied up with the ways it uses feelings and images; metaphors and jokes; rhyme and rhythm; stories and wonder; heroes and the exotic; hopes, fears, and passions; hobbies and collecting; and much else in engaging the imaginations of both teachers and learners with literacy. Literacy, and its associated cognitive tools, is one of the great workhorses of our culture, and it can greatly enrich the lives of those who learn to use it well. What this book does, then, is show how we might better teach our students to use this great cultural tool kit for their immediate, future, and everyday benefit.

Two Sources of This Approach

A part of the novelty of this approach is that it draws on the work of Russian psychologist Lev Vygotsky (1896–1934) and extends what he called cognitive tools for use in daily literacy instruction. What are cognitive tools, you may ask? The short answer is that they are *features of our minds that shape the ways we make sense of the world around us*; the richer the cognitive tool kit we accumulate, the better the sense we make. A slightly longer answer is that the term *cognitive tools* is commonly used to refer to what might more accurately be called *tools of imaginative engagement*. Several of the tools introduced later involve emotions and other features of thinking that are not products of the mind in the same way that metaphor and hyperbole are, for example. As used here, *cognitive* is a loose descriptor for the tools that engage our minds.

The particular tools we pick up influence our interpretations of the world around us, just as lenses influence what our eyes see. The lenses or cognitive tools mediate how we can see and make sense of things. If we want to understand how and what we can learn, then, we should focus our attention on those cognitive tools. Our educational challenge is how to stimulate, use, and develop these tools to enhance students' understanding and their literacy skills—and that's what this book aims to show you how to do.

Vygotsky's work (e.g., Rieber & Wollock, 1997; Vygotsky, 1962, 1978) suggests a new approach to teaching literacy, because his idea of how human beings develop intellectually is fundamentally different from the way we have been accustomed to think of the process in the West since the time of Jean-Jacques Rousseau (1712–1778).

Another source for this approach involves studies of thinking in traditional oral cultures. I recognize that this might seem a rather unusual place to look to for help with everyday literacy teaching today, but I hope you'll stick with me as we explore what this seemingly indirect route to literacy instruction has to offer. Clearly, children and adults in the West who come to literacy classes cannot be considered in any simple sense like people who live in oral cultures. For one thing, the environment of the modern nonliterate child or adult in the West is full of literacy and its influences. But despite this, many of the cognitive tools we find in oral cultures, such as storytelling and rhyming, help us to understand how literacy instruction might be made more imaginatively engaging to students. Even very briefly exploring some of the cognitive tools of oral language can yield a number of practical techniques.

Cognitive Tools in Everyday Teaching Practice

Teaching Literacy takes seriously the idea that there is an alternative way to think about how children learn, a way that is somewhat different from the traditional and progressive approaches that have dominated education for so long. This new approach leads readers down a different road from phonics, whole language, and even the more nuanced attempts to combine them, which are so prevalent today. You will learn what you can do in practice by developing the array of Vygotsky-inspired cognitive tools and how to adapt them for today's learners in light of recent research (Imaginative Education Research Group, 2005). Kept to a minimum, the theoretical underpinnings of this book's approach have been published previously (Egan, 1997).

Literacy Learners, Young and Old(er)

An oddity of this book is that it addresses literacy learning for both children and adults. These are commonly considered to be rather different fields. But in Vygotsky's terms, the cognitive tools we have—such as those that come along with oral language and with literacy—are crucially important in influencing learning. There will inevitably be some differences between nonliterate children and adults learning to read and write, if only due to the differences in the range of experience they have had. This is particularly true when those experiences have been frustrating for nonliterate adults and have made them resist further literacy learning. But this approach brings into focus the many more features children and adults have in common in learning literacy than have been typically recognized in the past.

The Cognitive Tool Kits of Language and Literacy

What do these cognitive tools look like?

In Part I we dive into the cognitive tools that are commonly found in oral cultures and that remain common today. Teachers can get a better grasp on how to help people learn literacy by understanding the tools that underlie it and from which it emerged historically and from which it emerges now. Examples of how each of these tools can be used in everyday literacy teaching will be applied to the following:

- *The story*—this is one of the most powerful tools for engaging the emotions in learning.
- *The flexible use of metaphor*—this is crucial for flexible and creative literacy.
- *Vivid images*—generating images from words is central to engaging the imagination in learning.
- *Binary opposites*—this is a powerful organizing tool, common to nearly all early childhood stories.
- *Rhyme and rhythm*—these are potent tools for aiding memory and for establishing emotional meaning and interest.
- *Jokes and humor*—certain jokes can help make language "visible" and greatly aid awareness and control of language.
- And some others are included, too.

These tools are most prominently used by children between the ages of three through seven. I offer an age range because different children in different circumstances differ in (1) the time it takes, (2) the degree of fluency, and (3) the control they develop in using these tools. These tools do not go away with literacy development, but literacy affects them in ways we explore in the second half of the book.

Part II focuses on the tools that move students from early acquisition to fluency. Here we focus on the two to four years *after* literacy instruction begins, when students come to read and write reasonably well but have not yet become at ease with more complex forms of literacy. As a result, the tools in Part II apply primarily to children from the ages of six through ten. Every teacher knows that the range of attainment in any class during these years is quite wide. While I've listed a small age range, keep in mind that the tools allow some latitude for their applicability, as you'll see. Frequent examples are given of how the following tools can be easily used in teaching literacy:

- *"The redefinition of reality"*(Bruner, 1988, p. 31)—in which students' interest in content shifts in subtle and important ways
- *Engagement by the limits of reality and the extremes of experience*—in which students develop a fascination with the exotic and extreme, as, for example, in the *Guinness Book of World Records* (2002)
- *Associations with the heroic*—which gives confidence and enables students to take on, to some degree, the qualities of the heroes with whom they associate
- *Seeing knowledge in terms of human qualities*—recognizing that all knowledge is human knowledge and a product of someone's hopes, fears, and passions, making the world opened by literacy more richly meaningful
- *Collecting items or developing a hobby*—grasping securely some feature of reality can stimulate many literacy activities
- *The sense of wonder*—capturing the imagination in the worlds that literacy opens up, both real and fictional
- And some others

At the conclusion of almost every chapter in the book is a section called "Teachers, Try It Out." These sections present readers with various challenges to apply the chapter's concepts in everyday classroom practice. Teachers are encouraged to give the challenges a go on their own, but those looking for additional help can find an extensive variety of possible applications in the Appendix.

Planning Frameworks Using Cognitive Tools

Part III demonstrates how the principles established earlier can be used to design frameworks to assist the teacher in planning literacy lessons and units. Sample frameworks are provided for teaching such everyday topics as homonyms and the use of the comma. These frameworks involve using many of the tools in combination. They might be seen simply as organized reminders of the tools the teacher can count on to engage the students' imaginations and emotions in the topics at hand.

Having begun this introduction with a bold declaration, I should finish it by more modestly noting that I don't envisage the practices and techniques I describe as displacing the many excellent practices and techniques currently in place. And, indeed, a number of items will be familiar, as they are already much used; for example, can we consider the use of the story as a new idea for teaching literacy? Of course not. Good teachers use a number of these practices intuitively. What I intend to show is how we might *routinely* achieve in the everyday classroom what currently requires rare intuition and energy.

The ideas and practices described in this book are also derived from the research and experimentation of the Imaginative Education Research Group, whose Center is at Simon Fraser University in British Columbia, Canada. You can find further material, and many more examples of lesson and units plans, on their Web site, at http://www.ierg.net. The names of the teachers and students you encounter in this book have been changed to protect their privacy.

Acknowledgments

One of the difficulties with this book grew out of my desire to provide lots of examples. I began to grow tired of my own voice and also recognized that many teachers might not approach planning the way I do. I thought the best solution would be to ask someone who had spent a number of years teaching to help me. As previously mentioned, in many chapters there is a section called "Teachers, Try It Out." In each of these sections there are two to three challenges for teachers to apply the pertinent ideas in ways that they could then use directly in teaching. I asked Gillian C. Judson if she would be willing to help me in this way, and she really took off, coming up with tons of examples I would never have dreamed of. The Appendix is taken up with Ms. Judson's responses to the challenges. I would like to thank her very much indeed. She has added a dimension to the book that makes it much more valuable.

I have also benefited from the kind, and occasionally very direct, comments from members of the Imaginative Education Research Group. In particular I would like to thank Sean Blenkinsop, Anne Chodakowski, Isabelle Eaton, Mark Fettes, Mark Frein, Natalia Gajdamaschko, Stan Garrod, Geoff Madoc-Jones, Ron McKellar, Andrew Schofield, and Rosalind Stooke.

Corwin Press wishes to thank Elena Bodrova and Katherine Taddie Kelly for their editorial insight and guidance.

About the Author

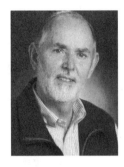

Kieran Egan is Professor of Education at Simon Fraser University in British Columbia as well as Director of the Imaginative Education Research Group. He has authored and edited over twenty books, many of which have been translated into European and Asian languages. In 1991, he won the prestigious Grawemeyer Award in Education for his book *Primary Understanding: Education in Early Childhood*.

Born in Clonmel, Ireland, Egan was raised and educated in England. He graduated from London University with a BA in History and from Cornell University with a PhD in Education. In 1993, he was elected to the Royal Society of Canada. He is a foreign associate member of the National Academy of Education and holds a Canada Research Chair in Education.

Part I

The Cognitive Tool Kit of Oral Language

Part I describes literacy teaching in a wider, more imaginative educational context than is sometimes evident in current teaching and in the exercises by which it is commonly performed. My aim is to show how we can design routine lessons and units that can really engage students with literacy activities. The information and examples offered don't represent some idealistic view; rather, they are dictated by pragmatic concerns for the achievement of efficient literacy.

CHAPTER ONE

Using the Story Form

Meeting Objectives by Engaging Feelings

Teaching literacy successfully requires us to engage the feelings of our students in what we want them to learn. In general, this may seem like a claim most teachers would agree with but perhaps with some hesitancy. When it comes to thinking about phonemes, comma use, or irregular plurals, engaging students' feelings in the topic might seem just a little—shall we say—optimistic, if not downright weird.

You may be wondering, then, why this book begins with a concept so seemingly improbable. I encourage you to read on, and you'll come to see that there's a good reason to deal first with feelings and emotions. But I must warn you—there's more. This approach asks you not only to engage your students' feelings, but also to find *within yourself* an emotional connection with the topic. If you have been teaching about phonemes and commas and plurals for ten years, the idea of getting emotionally turned on by such topics will perhaps seem weird indeed. But when considered for a few minutes, you might just agree that it makes perfect sense.

A routine part of the preservice education of nearly all teachers today is learning how to plan lessons and units of study—for teaching literacy no less than for any subject area. Most commonly, the teachers are instructed to begin this planning by stating their objectives for the lesson or unit: What do they aim to achieve? They are also taught methods for organizing the materials in order to effectively present the particular content to their students, directed always by their objectives. This general scheme of planning was devised in detail by Ralph Tyler in the late 1940s (Tyler, 1949) and was derived, according to the Tanners, from the earlier work of John Dewey (Tanner & Tanner, 1980).

It obviously makes sense to have clear objectives for one's teaching. But these strategies for planning teaching were derived initially from the procedures used in industrial processes for producing washing machines and automobiles (Callahan, 1962). The process went something like this:

- Design the final product—one's objective
- Organize the assembly line to construct the product bit by bit—one's methods
- Arrange supplies of the materials along the line—one's content
- Do testing to ensure that the product functions as planned—one's evaluation

These strategies represent one of the earlier and subtler influences of the corporate and industrial world on education. While there is obviously nothing wrong with planning procedures that help teachers organize and teach curriculum material more efficiently, there is a problem if those procedures fail to take into account something vital about education.

One of the differences between producing knowledge in students and producing washing machines and automobiles in factories is that knowledge becomes part of the living minds of students. It becomes tied into the meanings students then bring to make sense of the world and of their experiences. Crucially, it becomes tied into their emotional and imaginative lives. If we want to design and plan teaching in such a way that the emotions and imagination of students are engaged, then we might be wise to consider an approach that puts these features in their proper, prominent place. Let's begin looking at some of the cognitive tools preliterate students use so that we can find alternative categories for planning teaching, from which we can construct planning frameworks to help with the job.

Stories and Feelings

When we learn to speak a language, we gain not only the words and grammar but also an array of additional tools. One of the most pervasive is the story. Wherever we find oral language use, we also find stories. What is a story? What an odd question, in that everyone knows what a story is: It's a narrative that has a beginning that usually sets up some kind of conflict, a middle that complicates it, and an ending in which the conflict is resolved. But that doesn't seem to be such a big deal—at least not big enough to explain why all human cultures have used stories, and nearly all oral cultures have used them as central to their religious lives.

If we look a little deeper, we can see why stories are universally used in all human cultures and why you and I use them all the time, even when we might not recognize we are using one of the most ancient and powerful of all cultural inventions.

The Story Tool

So what kind of "tool" is the story? Well, it's the kind of tool that enables you to understand how to feel about events. Stories shape experience and knowledge into forms that can uniquely establish their emotional meaning. Stories don't simply convey information and describe events, they also shape their contents so that we will feel good or bad, joyful or sorrowful, as we hear about them. No other form of language can do this.

If I were to tell you about Anna Davidson, a generous and skilled doctor, and added, "It was a hot day, and she dived into the water," you may feel a small pleasure for her. But when I further tell you "the water was crowded with hungry sharks," you may feel some regret or distress. The story could continue with the information that she was trying out a new shark repellant or trying to save a child who had fallen in the water. Your feelings about her diving into the water would change, depending on the subsequent events. You would know you had reached the end of the story when you knew how to feel about her diving in and about the other events. In this case, our feelings would also be significantly shaped by whether the doctor later had or was lunch.

Now think for a moment about television commercials. You know that the break for the ads comes during a show, partway through its story, when you remain in doubt about how you should feel about the events you have seen so far. Certainly there are conventional and stereotypical endings that help us know that the story is concluded, but primarily our emotions are what tell us the story has ended. That's why we can't program a computer to recognize a story as distinct from any other kind of narrative: It lacks the emotional equipment that would allow it to *feel* meaning.

Using the Story Tool in a New Way

When people write about the use of stories in teaching literacy, they most commonly refer to fictional stories and discuss the many ways that stories can be used and their great educational power. Here we bypass the use of fictional stories and literature—not because they don't matter, but because there are already many fine books about this topic. Instead, we'll focus on a different use of the story, although inevitably we'll also refer to some fictional stories.

The great power of the story, for the purposes of literacy instruction, is that it can shape content of any kind, true or fictional, into emotionally satisfying forms. When a father asks his daughter, "What's the story on the new soccer coach?" or a mother asks her son, "What's the story on the new teacher?" the parents are not asking their children to make up a fiction. They are asking them to select events from their experiences and shape them to bring out their emotional meaning, to help the parents know how to feel about the coach or the teacher. We constantly use the story form to shape events, to tell our friends about something that happened in the office or an adventure on holiday. This ability to narrate is a central human skill, and those who do it well have both a satisfying ability to clarify and sharpen meanings for themselves and important power in being able to convey information and meanings to others. This power can be greatly valued in all walks of life. It is one of the great skills of orality (the cognitive tool kit of people who live in oral cultures), and its development can lead to an enriched literacy. It is also one of the great skills that can make teachers effective in educating.

Stories in the Classroom

For teachers, stories accomplish two important things simultaneously: Stories can communicate information very clearly and effectively, and they can engage the emotions of the students in the knowledge being learned. While the more general and powerful use of the story structure in planning and teaching will be seen in Part III, here we look at some smaller-scale ways in which we can bring stories into play.

Storyfying Literacy Tasks

There are endless ways the story can be integrated into teaching literacy. We'll begin with a very general use of the story, picking up from the idea of welcoming students to the wide community of readers and writers. Then, you'll see how even the most basic exercises can be made more meaningful and engaging by drawing on the story form.

It's helpful to start by telling students the true story of literacy itself, in which they are to become participants. The example that follows demonstrates one such way. Of course, both adults and children first coming to literacy instruction will have ideas about what literacy is and even how they will go about learning it. But few will know much about how literacy developed and reached the stage at which they will experience it.

Ms. Chou's Kindergarten Class

Ms. Chou started a kindergarten class in a very multiethnic neighborhood by talking about how people began writing as a way to keep a record of quantities. They would make an icon for one barrel, sack, or sheep, and two of the icons for two, and so on. Ms. Chou introduced the word *icon* and drew some examples on the board. The children seemed to grasp the concept easily, perhaps because of their exposure to computer icons.

The teacher then said she had made a different icon for each student in the class. She had drawn round bodies with stick arms and legs on the board, one for each child, in bright yellow, and had written the children's names under them. She then suggested that this system maybe wasn't such a good idea to help count. Because there were so many drawings to count, it would be just as easy to count the children each time anyone wanted to know how many there were. She then told them that long, long ago, people did make drawings like this on slates so they would know how many sheep they had. They could check days later to see whether they had lost any sheep or whether one might have been stolen.

Ms. Chou invented a shepherd named Tom who was worried he was losing sheep from his flock. Ms. Chou drew a very simple representation of a sheep.

She told the children that Tom got some slates and drew an icon like this for each sheep, all twenty of them.

By the time Tom had finished drawing, he had lots of slates, and it was quite a task to make sure he was keeping an accurate match of the number of real sheep against the number of sheep icons. Then, Ms. Chou explained, Tom's daughter, Mary, suggested that instead of making an icon for each sheep, he should make the icon and then put next to it a simpler *index mark* for each sheep—the index was a simple line, which she drew next to her sheep icon. So the daughter showed her father that he could have a sheep icon with twenty lines next to it, one for each sheep, and he could fit it all easily on a single slate.

The children all agreed that this was much more sensible.

During the rest of the class the children seemed spellbound as Ms. Chou described the next ingenious step, when the daughter told her father about a new system that she had heard about. This was the invention of using *symbols* for numbers. These symbols would replace the index marks. Ms. Chou showed how the daughter taught her father about this even easier way of keeping a record of how many sheep there were. She wrote "2" and "0" to replace the twenty index lines. So it became possible to record quantities of objects quite compactly in writing.

20

The class went at a slower pace than suggested here, of course. But by the end, when Ms. Chou asked the children whether they'd like to learn the symbols that Mary taught her father, the children were all eager to learn this neat trick, knowing of course that it was a trick every adult had learned how to use.

Ms. Chou didn't need to make up a complicated story in order to personalize the ingenuity involved in counting systems. After all, individual people long ago did invent these progressively more complex yet also more simple and effective tools for counting objects. Her simplified account of the historical development helped get over a common problem: many nonliterates assume that each word represents a thing. You can see this assumption among children learning to read today. If the teacher writes "Three little sheep," tells the children what the writing says, then rubs out one of the words and asks what the writing says now, many children will spontaneously say "Two little sheep" because two words are left on the board (Olson, 1994).

The remarkable story of literacy can be told in all its intriguing ingenuity in a manner that is easily engaging to students. The purpose of the story-form is to connect students' emotional commitment to that ingenuity and for them to see themselves as becoming a part of this remarkable adventure. (The foregoing example is extended in a later chapter to show how to use such an elaborated story to engage students' imaginations in literacy in general.)

But this is just using story as a general introduction. We can use it equally effectively for the simplest and most detailed practical activities. The stories we create do not need to be riveting, knuckle-whitening thrillers but, rather, can be quite simple accounts of people engaged in everyday activities. Obviously, the more entertaining we can make the stories, the better.

Mr. Rodda's Adult Literacy Class

Mr. Rodda wanted to show his class of adult literacy learners how to form plurals. Usually, teaching basic word features is taught mechanically, but it requires only a little thought to recast those activities into stories. Instead of simply giving the learners a list of singular words and asking them to write the plural forms, Mr. Rodda took a list of singulars and wrote them into a brief story. The students were then asked to recast the story using plurals. In Mr. Rodda's class, the word list included *woman, stone, my, he, I, boy, pencil, brother, paper, friend*, and *plant*.

Instead of putting the words in a column, with a blank space in which to write the plural, Mr. Rodda wrote a story in which he underlined the words he wanted the students to write in the plural. He asked them to write out the story again with plurals where he had underlined the singulars.

> A woman went down to the river to get some water for a plant that looked too dry. A boy sat on a stone with a pencil and paper. The woman asked the boy what he was doing. "I am writing to my brother," the boy said. "But you can't write," the woman replied. "That's all right," said the boy. "My brother can't read."

It's important to mention that when Mr. Rodda performed this activity with his class, fewer than half of the students could understand it in written form, as demonstrated. For most of the students, Mr. Rodda read the story, and the substitution of plurals was done orally.

To adapt this exercise for another literacy lesson, in which we wanted students to select from a set of words the best word to fill in blank spaces, the students might be more readily engaged if the blanks appeared in a simple story rather than in disconnected lists of sentences.

The foregoing example demonstrates one way to make a list into a story in a simple way. The form of the story used—drawing on another of the cognitive tools we'll discuss later—is the *joke*. You don't need to use jokes all the time, but they do lighten the learning load a little now and then, and our students at an adult learning centre in a Vancouver suburb certainly appreciated them. In fact, we learned that many of the students really looked forward to the classes because they knew they would hear a lot of jokes as they learned.

Much of the humor in the examples to follow, and especially in those found in the Appendix, is real "groaner" stuff. But it is exactly what really engaged our younger students, the four- and five-year-olds particularly.

Any of the routine exercises of early literacy that are usually presented by some drill method can be made more engaging and meaningful if put into a story context. Again, not *all* activities need to be story-shaped, and the challenge of inventing stories for all activities could be a little intimidating. Two points may be made with regard to this last concern:

1. With even a small amount of practice, it becomes easier to think of activities and exercises in story form. It is, after all, an older and more basic form of human thinking than almost any other we know of.

2. If these principles are found to be persuasive, no doubt many more materials will be published for teachers with story form examples.

Inventing Comic Characters

Any teacher can invent a stock comic character who has come from another country or another planet and is trying to learn about the local language and its written form. So whenever any new and complicated task is to be started in class, the comic character can be reintroduced and a story told to describe how he or she goes about learning it. Take the common English word ending, "ough." Our comic character, Bea Wildered, sees "ough" written in the word *through* and asks someone how it is pronounced. "Oo," she is told. She feels confident that she has learned this odd set of letters—until she hears someone talking about the bough of a tree. She asks how *bough* is spelled. "But that must be 'boo'!" she thinks. She is bewildered and walks towards a noisy demonstration where someone is carrying a sign saying, "We have had enough!" She wonders, "We have had 'enoo' or 'enow'?" When she asks a friend which one is right, she is told the word is pronounced "enuff." And so one can go on, with our character becoming gradually crazier as she begins to wrestle with the thor*ough*ly confusing English spelling and pronunciation, in which she still has to discover bought, cough, dough, hiccough, slough, and on and on. I have been told there is an *I Love Lucy* show in which Lucy's husband is trying to read to their son and running into just this "ough" problem.

The story here is simply a matter of having an invented character, a series of related incidents, and the character's emotional responses. One can—in cases where there is a rule or a common pattern (as in "i before e except after c")—have the character discover the rule or pattern and so avoid the punishment for misuse, whether it be as simple as humiliation or as extreme as a speedy retreat to the home planet, or whatever else the teacher and children determine. It would be important, of course, not to make the difficulties seem insurmountable!

The character can be made to suffer the same difficulties the students are to encounter and can be shown to be successful by recognizing in minor dramatic ways the particular lesson the teacher will then go on to reinforce with the students.

Personifying Elements of Language

Another option is to make the letters or phonemes become the characters in the story. Many first-grade children experience difficulty with phonemic awareness and are unable to remember that certain letters, when paired together, make a sound unlike either letter alone. The teacher could create a story to explain such anomalies. For example, one might tell a story like the following to explain the "th" sound:

> The Letters T and H don't get along very well. One day their teacher, Ms. Rules, caught the letter T sticking his tongue out at the letter H. She tried to get them to talk out their problems, but whenever they were together, one or the other was sticking his tongue out. All she could hear T saying was /th/ (as in "this"). Even H, who was usually rather quiet, started sticking his tongue out at T and saying /th/ (as in "thanks"). To this day, whenever T and H are together, they stick their tongues out at each other and behave very improperly—making sounds that sound nothing like the /t/ and /h/ sounds they are supposed to make.

After the story, the children could be asked to create an image in their minds (and possibly also on paper) of the two letters together sticking their tongues out.

Creating a Literacy Adventure

Stories can have even more imaginative and emotional engagement. One of the tricks of literacy is the recognition of words as arbitrary sounds that we have invented for our purposes. A pretend story can be set up, as Ms. Stewart did for her second-grade class, in which she and the class were explorers on a strange planet. They had discovered a weird building, and it had many rooms in it. Their job was to determine what the building was for and to describe it for the people back on their home planet, who were excitedly following their discoveries. She drew a rough sketch on the board. They had to decide what to call it, so Ms. Stewart suggested they simply name it *école*. But what was this *école* for? Once they got inside they saw it had many divisions, each of which they decided to call a *salle*. She drew some of these *salles*. Inside each *salle* were many small, rectangular objects that were hard on the outside but then had sometimes hundreds of white sheets stacked inside. They decided to call each of these stacked up objects a *livre*.

She had also brought into class with her some odd objects that she guessed none of the children would be familiar with—a small, flat electronic machine for weighing letters or food, a Russian samovar, a pyramid clock that had ceased to work, some old English pennies, and other bits and pieces. She invited groups of students to decide what they should call these things. She wrote the names on Post-it notes and stuck them on the objects. Between each of the names they invented, she added some more information about the strange place they were discovering—for instance, the walls had invisible but still solid parts, and she called each a *fenêtre*.

Nearly all the students found it easy to remember these words while they thought they were parts of their invented language.

This lesson continued for a few classes, and Ms. Stewart gave increasing clues that she and the class were not humans and that the strange planet they were visiting was Earth, that the building was a school, and that they had learned a fair amount of French vocabulary. She also spent some time discussing the marks she had put over *école* and *fenêtre*. At one point she showed how there were a lot of words that could be given to some things that were frequently used, but there wasn't much point naming other things that weren't differentiated in use. Also she explained that an overall name was useful for things that might look different but had similar functions, but particular names were also needed for each of them, so she gave a name for "coin" and then called the big ones "pennies" and added a few "centimes."

Ms. Stewart's story had two results:

1. The children were given a sense of how names are given to things largely depending on their uses.

2. The children were delighted to discover they had been learning French.

They asked that their adventures on the strange planet Earth be continued for quite some time, especially after they had explored some *maisons* by traveling along some flat and smooth *rues*. They also took particular pleasure in describing themselves as aliens, with a variety of tentacles, bug eyes, and exotic colors, which Ms. Stewart spent some effort illustrating.

It might seem that teaching students some French is not much help for their learning basic literacy skills in English, but you might reflect on the number of literacy skills that were being learned in Ms. Stewart's French lessons. (As you may have assumed, she set up their situation and their search for an inhabited planet in a more elaborate way than indicated in this much-abbreviated description.)

Teachers, Try It Out*

1. You are introducing the suffixes that indicate past tense. How can you fit this task into a story form?

2. You want to draw students' attention to detailed word forms, so you decide to design a class on recognizing words within words (e.g., "at" in "cat" or "ate" in "plate"). How can you fit this task into a story form?

3. You want to draw students' attention to differences between written and oral forms of language. How can you fit this task into a story form?

Final Words

This chapter has focused on one general sense of the story in teaching literacy. There are many common accessories that could be used in lessons like those described—dress-up props, puppets, pictures, story chair or rug, and so on. Again, they've not been mentioned here because there are many excellent books that describe this aspect of literacy teaching. Instead, this chapter has looked at bringing out the emotional and imaginative importance that is at the core of literacy as a human activity.

---

*In the Appendix there are suggested responses to these challenges as well as responses for every chapter in which there is a "Teachers, Try It Out" section.

When beginning to plan any literacy task, it would do no harm to ask, like the newspaper editor, "What's the story here?" That is, how can the topic be presented in a manner that brings out its emotional meaning and engages the students' imaginations? It isn't possible to be mesmerizingly successful at this all day, every day, of course, but it's a question that can help you to be a bit more imaginative and to find what is emotionally important about the topic personally as well as for the students.

Twenty years ago—good heavens!—I wrote a book called *Teaching as Story Telling*. The theme of that book, as of this chapter, was to show that thinking about lessons and units of study as good stories to tell, rather than simply as sets of objectives to attain, can help to bring some extra energy and interest into teaching and learning.

CHAPTER TWO

Images We Care About

Too, Two, and To

In this chapter, the word *images* does not mean pictures; instead, it refers to those constructs we form in our minds in response to things we hear or read. Consider the following:

> Jean arrived home after a long day in the office, exhausted by the dreary drive along the freeway. She made some tea and walked down the lawn past the flowerbeds to the Japanese garden. She sat on the steps of the teahouse, delighting in the curve of the tall bamboo as it bent gracefully over the pond, and she counted three new, yellow water lily flowers that had opening during the sunny day. The koi swam toward her, mouths opening and closing, demanding food. She tossed a handful on the water and sipped her tea, watching the stream wind through the stones and fall with water's irregular music into the pond.

We seem unable not to form images in our minds, however fleetingly, in response to such words; the images of a crowded freeway, a lawn through flowerbeds, the pond and its water lilies pass easily through our minds. The images are not simply quasipictures; you may also have formed an image of the sound of water falling. The images formed while listening to or reading a passage like the foregoing will be different for each of us. When we are provided a physical picture, this construction of our unique images is greatly limited and is the same for everyone. In a school context, it limits each student to the one shared representation. This is not to say that we should avoid using pictures! But it is to say that constantly providing pictures and allowing little practice for generating unique mental images is likely to discourage this aspect of the development of the imagination. TV and video games constantly provide children with stereotypical and somewhat clichéd pictures. I am not running a campaign against such things, but I do want to emphasize the alternative form of image generation to which we may give too little attention.

Images Aid Memory and Understanding

The currently dominant planning frameworks usually ask the teacher to begin by specifying what the students are to know or be able to do at the conclusion of the lesson or unit. These techniques focus the teacher's mind on concepts and content. If we look at the kind of material that most readily engages students' minds, there is another element very commonly prominent in their thinking—and that is the image.

It is extremely rare for the currently dominant techniques to ask teachers to consider what vivid images are central to the topic to be taught, yet we use images all the time, and they can be the most potent tools for aiding meaningful memorization. Think of the most powerful memories you have, of the most significant events in your life, what you recall from dramatic events, or even what you recall most clearly from your history or science classes from your own schooldays. These are most likely to come to the forefront of your mind in the form of images. Oddly, perhaps, in a world saturated with visual pictures, we tend to forget the importance of images in our learning and understanding.

In the days before paper was plentiful, from the ancient world until quite recently, students learned a number of potent techniques for memorizing. Most of them involved the creation of strange and vivid images that encoded the knowledge to be remembered. Relatedly, all the oral cultures of the world have built their folk tales and myth stories on images that have great power and meaning for the social group. Those advertisements you may see that offer to improve your memory in thirty days all rely on training you to connect what you want to remember to vivid images. Given this widespread knowledge of the great importance of using images for meaningful learning, they tend to be neglected in teacher preparation programs. To remedy their absence, this chapter demonstrates how images are one of the important cognitive tools that come along with language, a tool we can use in teaching literacy.

Incorporating Vivid Images in Lessons

So we might find it useful in our planning for teaching to spend time reflecting on what vivid and emotionally charged images are crucial to the topic. By "emotionally charged" I don't mean that they should be pulse-pounding, heart-throbbing images all the time, especially when what you're trying to teach is proper comma use. Rather, the emotional component of the image should be able to engage our feelings, even if in only a small degree.

Take a moment to think about topics like the past tense or comma use. We can begin by asking ourselves, what are they? What do they do for us? Who invented them? What purposes do they serve? These are basic and simple questions, even if the answers are not always simple to discover. Their purpose is to direct the mind toward what is most important about the topic at hand and especially toward its human meaning and importance. Immediately we can begin to think of how difficult life would be if words lacked tenses. We might also consider what words on the page would look like without commas.

Teaching Tenses

Our introduction to tenses might focus on their resourcefulness and convenience. We could then look for an opening to our unit that would highlight these qualities in some way that brings out emotion in children, such as sympathy and excitement.

> There was a woman who lived long ago, at a time before the invention of tenses. She had a word to say "I go" but because her language lacked tenses, it was unclear if this "go" referred to some journey she had already come back from or one she hadn't yet made.

With some vocal embellishment on the part of the teacher, children will likely be caught up in the story of this poor woman who was not able to communicate to others about her past or future travels.

Teachers can let children know that some people solved the woman's problem by adding words to their language, such as "I go yesterday" or "I go tomorrow." In fact, some languages still use such a manner of expressing tense. But for our woman who lived long ago, how much easier it would have been to say "I went" or "I'm going" or "I will go." Imagine how people responded to the person who first invented such a trick of language. For surely someone did. Others are likely to have taken it up quickly. And then it would have spread from tribe to tribe. Try to picture the incident and what it meant to people. It wasn't an earth-shattering invention, perhaps, but it has probably had more simple and beneficial influence, and has been used more widely, than most other inventions in history.

Understanding the Ingenious Comma

Similarly, the comma can bring to mind images representing such feelings as courtesy and delight at ingenuity. It's a very kind thing the comma does for readers, helping to chunk sensible parts of a sentence together so we can derive meaning, no matter how long a sentence may be. The ingenious comma is used primarily as an act of courtesy by the writer toward the reader, but it is an act of courtesy that has had a tremendous impact on human history. Making reading easy has transformed the world and encouraged the democratization of knowledge and all that has come with it. So an image that we can begin with could be of a large comma rising over the heads of history's great conquerors—Alexander, Caesar, Napoleon or others of their renown—clearly superior to them in its lasting impact on the world. Such an image helps to set up an emotional association between the student and the powerful, courteous, and ingenious comma.

Tying Concepts to Images

Some years ago, Sylvia Ashton-Warner (1972) developed educational ideas for children built on the idea that each child had his or her own particular concerns at any one time and one could find "key words" that would reflect these concerns. She was very successful in encouraging learning, and particularly literacy-based activities, by building them around the students' key words. Likewise, we can draw on images that are important for students—powerful images from their own childhood, of loved ones, or of important events, or from stories they have heard about princesses and kings, magic lands, monsters, witches, or whatever.

Nearly always, vividly recalled images are connected with strong emotions. Throughout the first few weeks of school, teachers should find a few minutes to spend with each student, one on one, and discuss images that are particularly powerful for them. From the images, the teacher and student might identify key words that help capture them to some degree. These words can then be written down for the student. Further work on literacy skills might be based on those key words, elaborating them by searching for synonyms, adding prefixes and suffixes that add to their flexibility in usage, ordering them alphabetically, and so on. Children's own keywords, derived from their own powerful images, provide a motivational factor and meaning often absent in contextless terms.

Key Word Images

Many of our teachers in Vancouver, British Columbia, began their students' first writing exercises by means of this key-words technique. Often they started with simple features in the students' environment. The children wrote their names and what they hoped to do, where they lived, and so on. Ms. McNeil augmented such writing tasks by encouraging students to also incorporate their key-word images, giving them, a beginning phrase such as: "I live in _____, which is _____," in which the first blank was to be filled in by the name of the place, and the second with their feelings about it.

Ms. McNeil then had the students take on a greater challenge by incorporating their images in a following sentence. The children spoke their sentences, and then Ms. McNeil wrote them down. The children produced such sentences as "My grandmother died on a sunny day," "I won the race in the rain," "The chickens ran into the road," "He broke my cup against the wall," "I sat by the river and listened to the birds sing" (from a child who lived in an inner-city high rise), and so on.

Human imagination grows by exercise in generating images from words. The mind is usually much more passive when observing pictures, particularly if they are on a TV screen. One can make a lot of exercises into image-forming activities. If dealing with color words, for example, a teacher can evoke an image of a man and woman talking on the street and ask the students, in their minds, to "color" their clothing:

"What color is the woman's skirt?"

"What color are the man's eyes?"

"What color is the man's shirt?"

"What color is the woman's necklace?"

The students might be encouraged to close their eyes as the scene is set up and to keep them closed as they imagine the colors. Then they write the color words and the name of the objects. They may have a pattern, such as "The _____ is _____." Depending on how advanced they are, one could provide them with the color and clothing words, allowing them to select and copy. They could compose the sentences themselves if more advanced.

Homophones

Can images help us teach students to distinguish homophones, like "to," "two," and "too"? Certainly. In this case, we can invent three friends, whose names are To, Two, and Too. We can invent a game in which each of the friends' personalities is somehow captured by their name. The children can be engaged in thinking about how the different forms of the words might capture their personalities. Deriving a personality from a word may seem a little bizarre, but it is a task that relies on an energetic use of metaphor (see the discussion to follow), and children can usually do this more easily than adults. Try it; you'll be surprised!

Introducing "Too"

Too is clearly very big, because he eats "too" much, he is also "too" tall, is clearly hyperactive, and always going beyond what is sensible. Unlike everyone else in his group, when he includes the letter "o" in his name, he has to include two of them.

Introducing "Two"

Two obviously does everything in pairs when she can—she has two cell-phones, two bikes, and is obviously overcareful: In case she might lose one thing, she always has a backup. It is clear from the spelling of her name that she really wishes she were a twin, as she's managed to put a "w" in her name, which makes it half way to "twin," even though there is no "w" sound in her name.

Introducing "To"

To is constantly on her way elsewhere or pointing to different things and places. She's clearly never satisfied with where she is or what she's got; she's a bit of a complainer. She's in so much of a hurry that, unlike the other two, she's dropped the third letter from her name and is the slimmest from all her hurrying.

Students can be encouraged to imagine characters based on the meaning of the word in such a way that they will likely remember them easily thereafter. To see a more elaborate version of this idea dealing with "there," "their," and "they're," go to http://www.ierg .net/teaching/lesson_unitplans.html.

Once the class has developed three distinct characters who capture something about the differences between *to, two,* and *too,* the teacher can begin to explore these differences by composing a story in which all three figure, perhaps with the students. The trick would be to build into the story *the deeper understanding of language and literacy* that can come from grasping how the same sound can perform three different linguistic roles, depending on context, and how literacy enables the eye to see immediately which of the three is intended. The plot could involve the three characters' irritation at constantly being confused, even though they think the differences among them would be obvious if people only knew them.

From Images to Letter Representation

How can we use images to help students begin to understand how writing works? One way is to provide images of how and why some central features of everyday texts occurred in history. The teacher might help the students to visualize writing in odd ways to better show how text functions. The following ideas might be spread over many lessons, but they're compacted here.

The Man and the Bus

The teacher (this could be you, but let's call her Ms. Stevens) begins by telling students a story about a man trying to get onto a very crowded bus. She asks the children to picture the bus in their minds. What color is it? Can they imagine the people sitting inside and then lots of standing people and a further crush of people by the door? How are they dressed? It is evening, you might say, and the people are going home from work. They all would like to get home as quickly as possible. How might they be behaving? Are they pushing? Are some impatient? Then she tells the story:

The bus was packed. When another man tried to get on, the people who were squashed around the door refused to let him in.

"It's too crowded. There isn't any more room," they said.

"But you must let me on," he pleaded.

"Why should we? Who do you think you are—someone important?" they shouted.

"No," he said. "I'm just the driver!"

Before the class, Ms. Stevens typed the joke story out, in capital letters, without spaces or other punctuation. She was careful to make the letters very big, maybe 48 pt. This is what it might look like—though these are only 16 pt. letters:

THEBUSWASPACKEDWHENANOTHER
MANTRIEDTOGETONTHEPEOPLE
WHOWERESQUASHEDAROUNDTHE
DOORREFUSEDTOLETHIMINITS
TOOCROWDEDTHEREISNT . . .

Earlier she had printed out two copies of the story, cut the text from one sheet into separate lines, and then stuck the lines together to make one long strip in which the letters just went on and on. The finished strip was around seven or eight feet long. It could be curled up and held neatly with a small elastic band or a paper clip.

Ms. Stevens discusses the joke for a few minutes with the students and then says that she wants to show them how such stories might be written. She then picks up the curled strip and gives one end to a reliable student to hold tightly. She gradually unrolls it until she has the whole strip open so that all the students can see it. Asking another student to hold her end of the strip, she walks back to the beginning of the long strip and, following the letters with her finger, reads the story again.

Thanking the students holding the strip, she takes it back and rolls it up again. She asks the students, "Is there another way you can think of in which we can write the letters down that tell the story?" Someone will mention a sheet of paper or a book. She can then hold up the sheet on which the story is written in sequential lines. "That's better. We don't have to carry around a roll, and we can stack the letters in lines like this. Does this look like any books you have seen?

What's the difference?" There will be some discussion, and the teacher can hold open a typical storybook so the students can more easily identify differences.

Going to the writing board she can start writing the capital letters from the sheet onto the board, sounding out the letters and then the words, though still making no separation of words when writing. She might write a little laboriously, taking the marker from the board after each letter. "This writing is slow work! It will take me a long time to write the whole joke down. But long ago, before there were computers, or typewriters, or any way to print words, people had to write everything by hand. It took such a long time, and was very difficult to read" (holding up the sheet of capitals again).

"Imagine that you wanted to write a very long story this way. It would take ages! But long ago, that's how people did it, until one day a clever monk had some ideas to make writing faster and easier to read. Here's what he did first." Ms. Stevens then writes out in capitals, "THE BUS WAS PACKED," sounding out the letters and words and then reading it a couple of times, pointing to the text. "That's easier to read, when the words are separated like that. But it still takes a long time to write. Now another monk, whose name was Alcuin—can you say that?—had another good idea to speed up the writing. Instead of doing it all in these big letters, he had the idea of making smaller letters that could slide together in writing, so you don't have to take the pen from the paper after each letter." She then writes, "The bus was packed," at much greater speed.

She also has a sheet of paper with the story typed in a regular, modern form in a large enough font size to fill the page. "Do you see any of the big letters like on the first sheet?" she asks, holding both pages up. "Yes, at the beginning of the lines sometimes. So when people first invented writing, they had only one alphabet of big letters, but to speed up writing, people like Alcuin invented a second alphabet. So each letter comes in two forms—a big, slow form and a quick, small form. So you can thank Alcuin for doubling the amount you have to learn. But you can also thank him for making it faster to write and also easier to read."

Ms. Stevens (or you) can ask the students if they know what a monk is. Can they imagine what Alcuin might have looked like? What did they write in those olden days? This can be a very informal discussion, but it is all designed to create images in the students' minds connected with the development of writing and give them some idea of why it has taken the form we are so familiar with today.

It might be useful to have some pictures of old manuscript pages to show them—not so much the great "illuminated" pages, but the more common crammed pages that are very difficult to decipher. (The Internet provides numerous examples, of course.) The aim is to help the student see writing not only as an exercise in deciphering the typical page of simple text, but also to see it in a context of the great adventure of making writing a wonderfully efficient system in which text is made hospitable to the eye. These are topics that will be revisited again later in this book.

Teachers, Try It Out

1. Compose a story about homophones—like to, two, and too— that brings out their distinct meanings through creation of personalities that are a reflection of the separate words and their meanings.

2. How can images help you and your students explore compound words, particularly how they sometimes reflect the meaning of the distinct words put together (e.g., "bedroom") and sometimes produce somewhat new meanings (e.g., "footlocker").

3. How can you encourage writing activities by building on emotionally charged images?

Final Words

Often when we provide terms and contexts for exercises, we can increase engagement by encouraging students to imagine them and draw on those images. As students discover how literacy can be used both to capture their images and also to elaborate on them, they develop some sense of the unsuspected, incidental pleasure and power literacy can provide. Our students all bring a wealth of mental images with them to class, many of which hold great emotional importance for them. It would be a pity to try to teach literacy while ignoring the massive resource of images—which, in the end, literacy is going to influence and be influenced by.

CHAPTER THREE

Binary Opposites

Goldilocks and Civil War

We've already seen one aspect of the currently dominant principle of teaching methodology: that we should always begin with what students are already familiar with and then introduce the new knowledge we want them to learn that is associated with it. The sensible idea behind this is that students should be able to enlarge their knowledge along lines of gradually expanding associations from the known to the unknown. This is assumed to make the process easier and more logical and so make the new knowledge more comprehensible.

The problem with this logical principle comes when it is taken as the only way in which new knowledge can be meaningfully introduced. And this is how it is often represented in textbooks. When planning a new topic, teachers are commonly instructed to first find something associated with the topic with which the students will be familiar. I recall a student teacher who had to begin teaching the Middle Ages. She was despairing because all the content she was reading seemed so different from her students' experience. How could she connect them with it? Eventually, she triumphantly announced that she had found the connector: the period in which women first wore high-heeled shoes!

The trouble with using such a principle is that it easily leads to such triviality. It hides the obvious fact that students can be connected with the Middle Ages through the emotions they share with those who lived, loved, feared, struggled, fought, and engaged their passions in that era's actions and events.

Using Opposites to
Expand Upon Understanding

The other trouble with working only from the familiar is that it hides another principle of learning commonly evident in children's thinking before literacy takes over their minds. Consider the kinds of stories young children, and adults, most enjoy. Under the surface of the narrative, we can nearly always locate two forces in conflict:

good–bad,

courage–cowardice,

security–fear,

friendship–hatred,

and so on.

This tendency to divide the world into opposites in order to make initial sense of things has been observed so commonly that we can easily take it so much for granted that we cease to notice it. Bruno Bettelheim (1976) observed that "[children] can bring some order into [their] world by dividing everything into opposites" (p. 74).

The point of this principle of learning is not to teach that things are made up of opposites, of course. But, rather, it is to recognize that such oppositions are a part of the tool kit of oral language and that teachers can expand understanding not only by gradual associations with what is known but also by mediating between opposites. Children may begin with characters who represent good or bad but soon learn that sometimes people are both good and bad. A whole range of mediating categories can be learned from the oppositions with which we can begin, and on those oppositions we can build any content we want. It will be made meaningful to the students not by previous familiarity but by the underlying emotionally charged binary opposites that they know profoundly. So we can immediately begin with characters and situations unfamiliar to children—such characters as talking middle-class bears, star warriors, witches, dragons, robots like Star Trek's Lieutenant Commander Data, or galaxies long away and far ago—and be confident children will understand.

The importance of this point will emerge as we look at examples. But it should be clear that using binary opposites and mediating between them can help us avoid the dogmatism of always moving along lines of associations from the known to the unknown, and it can also enable us to introduce new topics in dramatic ways that easily grab students' imaginations.

Using Opposites for Deeper Comprehension

We can also use opposites as a means to get to a deeper level of meaning than is sometimes easy to do.

Goldilocks and the Three Bears

For example, the teacher might use the attraction of patterns and oppositions in exploring just about any fairy tale with children. Take *Goldilocks and the Three Bears*. After telling the story and talking about it relatively freely, following children's interests and questions or comments, the teacher might ask the children what opposites they can think of in the story. The children might recall, with or without a bit of prompting, the porridge being "too hot" and "too cold," and the chairs and beds being "too soft" or "too hard." The porridge and chair and bed that are "just right" are baby bear's each time, of course. The teacher might ask whether the children can see opposites in the characters. After some discussion, the boldness of the (human) child and the considerateness of the well-behaved (animal) child are set in contrast. Goldilocks' disregard for others and the bear parents' concern for their child are also contrasted. Those observations may be enough for an interesting discussion of what is going on in the story—though the teacher could push further by picking up on the oddity of the nature-culture division, in which the natural animals are seen to be innocent and the human child is guilty, though unpunished. (The Goldilocks version we tell today comes from the later nineteenth century. In earlier versions the human interloper is seen to be punished.)

Finding Opposites in Common Terms

For a different kind of example, adult students might enjoy exploring how many opposites they can find stuck together in common terms and reflect on how they work. What do we mean by old news, civil war, inside out, voice mail, industrial park, half naked, loose tights and tight slacks, or criminal justice? One might give them the task of keeping a list of such terms. This helps the students notice language in a new way, and they can be encouraged to consider the meanings behind terms they may hear, like nonworking mothers, military intelligence, peace offensive and war games, random order, and so forth.

Mediating Binary Opposites

When students have familiarity with a number of binary opposites, teachers can then call attention to them to help make sense of stories and concepts. Teachers commonly teach binary opposites by providing students with two lists of words and asking them to draw a line linking the opposites. So the lists might look like this:

good	in
big	poor
brave	bad
high	cowardly
out	little
rich	low

But we can then introduce more fundamental oppositions, such as the ten that Pythagoras considered fundamental to the structure of the world: limited-unlimited, odd-even, unity-multiplicity, right-left, masculine-feminine, still-motion, straight-curved, light-dark, good-bad, square-rectangle. The teacher could write one side of the list on the board for the students initially and discuss their guesses at the opposites. Then the students might be asked to generate similar, very basic oppositions that they have observed, like rich-poor, happy-sad, wet-dry. Keep in mind that these kinds of exercises can be made more engaging by combining them with other cognitive tools, as we see with the humor and jokes section to come or the story tool discussed in Chapter 1.

Another activity might involve distinguishing which letters represent sounds made with the lips pressed together as opposed to those that represent open-mouthed sounds. Any other type of sound might be chosen to help establish a connection of letter symbol and sound.

Making Sense of Stories in Mr. Lee's Class

Mr. Lee used a technique designed to have students in his adult education class find the underlying binary opposites in stories he would tell them. The stories were not elaborate at all, just brief anecdotes he found in the paper or that he made up in the car on the way to work. One story, a combination of a piece he remembered from the paper and retold, went like this:

> Steve Nash was the first Canadian to win the National Basketball Association's award for Most Valuable Player. He used to be a skinny kid from Victoria, British Columbia, whom no one expected to become a sports star. He is the only non-American to win the MVP award. Nash received his award with his usual modesty. He is "only" 6 foot 3 inches in a game where most players tower above him. He did not play basketball until late in high school, and then his ambition to play in a major NBA team was taken as a foolish wish by everyone except his mother. He is far from the most skilled player in the league, but he works hard and is consistent.

After Mr. Lee told this story in class, students came up with a variety of oppositions: modest-boastful, rich-poor, no expectation–triumphant achievement, big-small, naturally skilled–constantly working, Canadian-American (which some students saw as opposites!), late start–early achievement, and most of them expressed in one way or another the emphasis built into the story of the unexpected rise of the modest person to heroic achievement.

Making up such a story might seem a daunting task. I think we are often persuaded to believe we are not able to do something because we are not encouraged to practice it. Mr. Lee said that he was at first concerned that he would have to find such stories all the time, as he imagined he couldn't compose them himself. But after he had used them for a little while and then made up a couple of his own, it proved easy to generate them. It was just a matter of thinking in a slightly different way and needing a little bit of practice. Also he was astonished to find that nearly every newspaper story had a wealth of such oppositions built in as a device to attract and hold readers' attention.

The use of abstract binary opposites can come into greater play in the overall planning of lessons or units. Later I show how they are central to one of the frameworks I describe.

Recognizing Truth From Fiction in Ms. Eaton's Second-Grade Class

Ms. Eaton also used items from newspapers in her Grade 2 literacy lessons. She used them in a variety of ways, but one of them, developed after we had discussed using opposites, involved her choosing odd and funny filler stories she'd found. Sometimes she would build in impossible or very unlikely items, though some of the true stories were unlikely enough. She would ask the children whether the story she told them was true or false. Then she asked those children who took a clear position for one or the other which features of the story made them believe it to be true or false. It wasn't long before all the children understood some of the criteria for deciding one way or the other. She commonly told one such story a day and took only about ten minutes or so to discuss it. It quickly became an activity the children looked forward to, and she found it quite challenging to come up with stories that were clearly either true or false but with clues that were not so obvious.

Recognizing Alphabet Letters in Mr. Tyers's First-Grade Class

Mr. Tyers used the attraction of patterns and oppositions in helping his Grade 1 students recognize the letters of the alphabet. He asked students which letters can be divided in half into equal parts and which cannot. And is there a change in the number of those equally divisible when capitals are considered—as in "h" to "H?" How about if the letters are sliced horizontally as distinct from vertically? How many letters can be successfully sliced into equal opposites both ways? Such activities help the eye begin to take over some aspects of recognizing language from the ear.

Teachers, Try It Out

1. Stick a large sheet of paper on a wall of your classroom. What kinds of activities could you invite students to perform using oppositions and mediation?

2. How might you ask students to tell a story from their own experience in a way that builds on opposites and mediation?

3. After students have read or listened to many stories in a particular genre (fairy stories, family tales, monster stories), how could you use oppositions and mediation to explore those stories and that genre more fully?

Final Words

Some of the teachers I've worked with were initially reluctant to try out this particular tool. Some said that they didn't want to encourage the children to see the world in terms of opposites, and they were especially wary of using such opposites as good-bad. They felt that it led to stereotyping and simplifying, when the aim of education was to give children a more complex view of things. Also, they said, nothing was simply good or bad and no one was simply courageous or cowardly; that such opposites were always mixed in some degree.

We spent some time discussing this and indeed agreed that certain kinds of stereotyping in fairy tales could have bad results, especially the consistent association of male with active and female with passive. The main point I was concerned to emphasize was that this tool was not one that we were creating for children but, rather, that it seemed to come along with language; it was there whether we liked it or not. Children and adults all tend to break down our experience and what we know into oppositions to get an initial conceptual grasp on it. Thereafter we can mediate between the oppositions to elaborate and complexify our view. It would be silly to ignore a tool that seemed to be used by all children to make sense of the world around them.

We also discussed the use of oppositions in fairy tales at length. Those of us defending the continued use of such tales argued that the presence of harmful stereotypes wasn't a good reason for banning them. Recognizing this tool provided a means to bring these hidden opposites to the surface and allowed us to explicitly discuss them with the students. This tended to be the approach that most teachers took, whether with fairy tales for children or newspaper stories with adults. In fact, this tool alerted the teachers to the previously missed hidden messages of many stories and allowed them to raise them for discussion in class, at a level appropriate to the students.

CHAPTER FOUR

Literal and Metaphoric Talk

"Like a Spring-Woken Tree"

When someone talks about growing old by saying, "I think I'm heading in the wrong direction," we can easily recognize what is meant, even though the language more commonly refers to making a mistake while traveling. We call this form of language *metaphoric*: referring to one thing in terms derived from another. It can, when used with wit, enlarge our understanding of the new process or situation it is referring to. We easily forget that most of our language use is vastly metaphoric. There is something decidedly odd about metaphor. Its enormous fluidity allows meanings to expand and slip and slide in all kinds of ways. It is clearly connected with creativity in thinking. Being able to use metaphor flexibly and fluently and in a controlled way is also central to becoming literate in more than the most limited sense.

It is also clear that young children have no difficulty recognizing the meanings of metaphors they may have never heard previously. I recall as a child at a movie hearing one character saying of another, "He bit the dust," and understanding immediately what was meant, even though the literal meaning would give no obvious clue to the intended meaning. And this is one of the easier examples of how we can grasp metaphors in early life. The strange near-miracle of language development we see in each young child not only is tied to the common statistics we read about how many words per day a child picks up between ages three and six but also is more miraculously tied up with the vast range of metaphors young children recognize and generate—and the fact that they can recognize them at all.

Recognizing and Reflecting on Language

One feature of good literacy, even early in the learning process, derives from being able to see language as an object, not just a behavior. Being able to see and reflect on language is crucial to gaining power in its use. One dimension of this ability is in not only recognizing and generating metaphors but also in being able to recognize them *as* metaphors.

Mr. Madoc, for example, gave a "metaphor of the week" prize. He set up a blank sheet of paper on a wall, and students were invited to either recognize a good metaphor someone used or to invent their own, and write them there. If students were unable to write the metaphor themselves, they would tell it to Mr. Madoc, who would write it for them. Within a few weeks, he had to find a much larger sheet of paper, as the students' examples quickly increased in number and cleverness. At the end of each week, a vote was taken for the best one. This relatively simple activity achieved an increase in the students' understanding of metaphor as well as their conscious awareness of language, and it clearly developed their "metalinguistic awareness." They also found it fun.

In the tool kit of language, metaphor is a powerful cognitive tool. In this approach to learning literacy, recognizing, generating, and manipulating metaphors is important. While the topic of "metaphors" may be a part of many literacy programs, it plays an unusually prominent role here. Also, while some teachers might think this topic rather difficult for youngsters, research on children's grasp of metaphor suggests that four-year-olds are better at recognizing and generating metaphors than most adults (Gardner & Winner, 1979).

Similes

The range of uses for metaphor in teaching is enormous, so to begin, let's focus on the kind of metaphor we call the *simile*. Obviously the teacher will want to make clear how a simile is different from the commonest sense of metaphor, even though it is itself a kind of metaphor. Usually a simple comparison example makes clear how the simile works—"My heart *is like* a spring-woken tree"—whereas a basic metaphor substitutes one term for the other: "My heart *is* a spring-woken tree."

Similes commonly follow the phrase "is like" and invite us to see one thing in terms of something else. I referred earlier to research indicating that preliterate children are better able to generate and recognize metaphors than literate adults. While I am not aware of research comparing this ability between literate and nonliterate adults, I would expect its greater use by the nonliterate, if only because they are less influenced by the "literalness" that literacy can encourage. And even if there is no significant difference, the fact that metaphor is a universal feature of language points to grounds for more explicitly using it in literacy programs. A literacy in which metaphor remains lively is better than one in which it does not.

Teachers associated with the Imaginative Education Research Group (IERG) had their students complete sentences beginning with these phrases:

"My home is like a . . ."

"Where I live, people work like . . ."

"My friend can sing like . . . "

"The end of the work (or school) day is like . . ."

The teachers also chose many more examples related to the context of the particular students' lives. The aim was for the student to find as many words as possible to fill in each blank. Depending on their stages in their literacy programs, they could write them or the teacher might write them. Some of the examples could be functional, related to the students' daily activities. Others might explore their emotions. For example, "When I am happy (sad), my heart feels like . . ." Our students were encouraged to use phrases as well as words to fill in the blanks.

Earlier in their programs, the teachers provided students with a set of words and invited them to choose those that they thought worked best in such examples as "I am as happy as . . ." The students could indicate all that seemed appropriate. Oddly, it tended to work better with unlikely examples, such as a camel, a postcard, a nose, a songbird, a fish, a new dress (shirt), a tree. It was as though the oddity, or the "distance" over which the metaphorical connection had to be made, stimulated their minds. Students often went far beyond the stereotypical expectations we teachers have as appropriate responses to that simple phrase. Some were clearly just wild, and the students found it hard to indicate what they had in mind, but others were clearly unexpected and effective, sometimes grounded in their own ethnic backgrounds.

Metaphors

Ms. Parrass instituted a "metaphor time" in her second-grade class. It usually lasted only about ten minutes each day, but quite quickly the children looked forward to it. At the beginning of the year, she would give the children a word in a simple phrase, a little like the simile exercise, and ask them, in pairs, to come up with as many metaphors as they could. They might be given a phrase such as "My heart is . . . ," and they would be given ten minutes—usually quite a noisy time—to write words that could complete the short sentence in unusual and interesting ways. Each pair of children would generate at least four or five answers, and some would produce as many as a dozen. They often seemed to be restricted by writing rather than by ideas. So we had answers like—just to choose some of the more unusual and effective—"a house," "a thorn," "a mouse," "a sky," "a battle," "an ocean," "a bird," "a gray stone," and, for reasons we couldn't quite figure out, "a potato."

Later, in the second year, the students were given a strip of paper with a sentence written on it. The sentences were always quite simple and straightforward. One example was, "The dog ran along the street, passed the car, and jumped into the garden." The challenge for the children was to make up as many metaphors as possible while keeping the meaning clear, though it must be admitted that meaning was occasionally sacrificed to some wild metaphors! The children worked in pairs again. At the end, the class voted for the best metaphors.

James and Alex came up with

> The barker roared along the car space, zipped the four-wheeler, and skyed the fence into the flowers.

Teresa and Dawn produced

> Fido legged it along the blacktop, passed the people-mover, and flew into the flowerbeds.

Mark and Sarah offered

> The paws padded along the tarmac, overtook the metal box, and soared into the veggie patch.

Aline and Jacob gave us

> The canine galloped along the dead earth [we thought this was an unusual and effective metaphor for a "street," where nothing grows], passed the metal chariot, and flew into the tamed plants [which we thought was also pretty good].

These examples give a flavor of what this group of children routinely produced. And I've corrected occasional spelling errors.

We had some fun exploring the common metaphors students heard on TV, having them figure out how they were derived. "Couch potato," "road hog," "feeling blue," "boiling mad," "deep secret," "bubbly personality," and a bunch of others gave the students lots to explore and talk about.

Teachers, Try It Out

1. How might you use metaphors to help students see the classroom differently?

2. One of the funnier uses of language occurs when people mix metaphors in a sentence, jumping from one metaphor to another wholly inconsistent one. For example, "He stepped up to the plate and grabbed the bull by the horns." A metaphor derived from baseball becomes confused with something a cowboy might do. "That wet blanket is a loose cannon," "Strike while the iron is in the fire," or (said by a school administrator whose budget was slashed) "Now we can just kiss that program right down the drain." What activity could you design so that students could consciously construct mixed metaphors and have some fun in the process?

3. How might you help students explore the most common forms of language they hear—on TV, via MP3s, and in their own interactions—by focusing on metaphor?

Final Words

A focus on metaphor expands students' minds beyond the routine and literal. We will not want to do this all the time, of course, but for an enlivening ten-minute change of pace, it can be valuable. It can also help to expose something important about language—that we can use it in our own ways to express our unique view of things.

There is no right answer to "My heart is . . . "; there is an indefinite number of right answers, and each student can be encouraged to find his or her own. But also, students learn that an important part of using effective metaphors is that they can be understood by others, even if occasionally one might need some explaining. Indeed, explanations can be powerfully educative moments. I recall vividly a group of students explaining why they had chosen to say that their heart was a thorn.

Aristotle, who was no fool, in discussing the business of writing well, noted, "The greatest thing by far is to be a master of metaphor."

CHAPTER FIVE

Jokes

Drawing the Drapes

Joking is not a topic often discussed in books about teaching literacy. At best it might be mentioned as a way of lightening up lessons. But I think it is of much greater importance than has usually been recognized. When we see something pretty well universal among language users, we should be alerted to the fact that it is of great importance, even though that importance may not be readily obvious. Nearly all children enjoy jokes, often extravagantly. Why? We don't need jokes to live adequately. What is going on? What are jokes?

Well, I'm not going to answer the last question here, nor could I answer it anywhere, but I do want to make one simple observation about the kinds of jokes that children (and adults) commonly find funny: These are the jokes that rely on taking the meaning of a word the wrong way. You know a thousand of them, probably, though perhaps you haven't thought of them in these terms.

Anne: "Whenever I'm down in the dumps, I buy new clothes."

Gillian: "So that's where you get them!"

or

Teacher: "Where are you from, Geoffrey?"

Geoffrey: "California."

Teacher: "What part?"

Geoffrey: "All of me."

or

Michael: "Dad, what are those holes in the new shed?"

Dad: "They're knotholes."

Michael: "Of course they are holes. I can put my finger through them."

These simple (and old!) examples rely on Gillian choosing to understand "down in the dumps" differently from the sense meant by Anne, Geoffrey misunderstanding whether the second question referred to the "where" or the "you" in the first question, and Michael misunderstanding the meaning of "knot" as "not."

The joke forces us to recognize something about the way language works. At the very least, we recognize that it's a slippery business, not some crisp, logical activity in which meanings are clear and nailed down. Basically jokes help us begin to see language, and literacy, as objects. The recognition of language as an object is crucial to becoming better able to manipulate it and use it with increasing flexibility. So any sensible program of literacy instruction will not use jokes simply as a trivial hook to attract students' attention; rather, it will recognize humor as a *constituent* of adequate orality and literacy.

Joking and "Seeing" Language

Many adults and children approach literacy classes with appropriate seriousness, and often, in the case of adults with particular vocational motivations, with a kind of grimness. But all human beings are amenable to the value of humor. And humor and seriousness of purpose are not in any way at odds with one another. A classroom within which humor is commonly used in exercises is a more pleasant place to be than one in which it rarely appears. One of the great gifts of literacy is access to pleasures that are available only through texts—and introduction to literacy, even if the motive is purely utilitarian, should show that there is also pleasure, that might, over the course of a literate life, far outweigh the simple utility.

Letter Recognition

There are endless ways in which one can help make even the very basic acquisition of *letter recognition* humorous. Again, these examples are not intended to displace the usual forms of teaching but can be drawn on to supplement them. The following are examples that most of our teachers used in one form or another.

There are a number of variations on the old

YY U R
YY U B
I C U R
YY 4 me.

This may puzzle the students. "What is the first letter?" the teacher might ask. "Y." Why, why? No, two Y's: "too wise."

Too wise you are
Too wise you be
I see you are
Too wise for me.

If this works, one might use the following conversation in a restaurant.

"F U NE X ?"
"S V F X"
"F U NE M?"
"S V F M"
"OK L F M N X"

A clue to interpreting this, apart from knowing and sounding out the letters, may be given by slowly reading the first line: F = have, U = you, NE = any, X = eggs. The customer in the last line happily orders ham and eggs. (It works better with some accents than others!)

Punctuation

When doing exercises on punctuation, the teacher might help students understand the effects of certain forms by giving them examples of sentences whose meaning changes radically (and funnily) depending on the punctuation used. "Private! No swimming allowed!" means something quite different when punctuated as "Private? No. Swimming allowed." Similarly, "I'm sorry you can't come with us" means something different from "I'm sorry. You can't come with us." Or, "The butler stood at the door and called the guests' names" is radically changed, by a tiny difference of punctuation, to "The butler stood at the door and called the guests names." The section at the end of most chapters of this book would have a different meaning if written "Teachers try it out!"

Humor in Amelia Bedelia

The popular children's book character Amelia Bedelia is a good example of making use of the humor that occurs when idioms are taken for their literal meaning, and it's a great choice to use in class. You may recall that when Amelia is asked to "draw the drapes," she sits down and attempts the task by sketching on a pad of paper. When she's asked to "prune the hedges" she promptly places prunes all over the shrubbery. If she is asked to take out the trash, she might take the garbage to a movie. If she is asked to "ice the cake" she will rush to the freezer to find the ice-cubes. Whenever there is a second possible meaning, Amelia is sure to take that one. After the initial laugh the stories are sure to bring, the class could discuss Amelia's mix-up and why it occurred. When teaching idioms or double meanings in the class, Amelia books or an invented character with similar confusion can make the material more interesting.

Reading Puzzles

One can introduce simple reading tasks such as puzzles in which interpretation reveals the humor. Take this sign that was next to a rail to which one might hitch an animal:

TOTI
EMUL
ESTO

Even the most literate might have some difficulty with this, and it can be used in the story of the history of literacy. It illustrates how writing commonly appeared soon after the invention of the alphabet and before the introduction of that basic item of punctuation—the space between words. Once you see it as "To tie mules to," you can appreciate the humor of how the simple meaning was so easily disguised.

Apart from these letter jokes, most literacy tasks can be put into the context of a joke equally as easily as into a list or other contextless exercise. The joke, of course, is a story, and the earlier comments made refer to jokes as well. As our work with the group of literacy teachers continued, I was not too surprised to discover that they had each begun to form a small collection of joke books from which they were frequently pulling ideas on which to build examples for all kinds of skill development lessons.

Teachers, Try It Out

1. How could you use jokes or humor to encourage students to recognize that real comprehension involves predicting later sections of the text on the basis of what they have already read?

2. How can you use jokes to help students with spelling?

3. Design a strategy for routinely using humor in teaching vocabulary expansion.

Final Words

"A scarecrow won a prize for being outstanding in its field." There are a number of theories about jokes and why they work, including Freud's notion of releasing tensions, though that one is a bit difficult to get the mind around. One simpler theory is based on the idea of incongruity: Jokes will only work in a community that understands the normal conditions and expectations in which the joke is set, and the joke works best by seeming to fit the normal expectations but tweaking one element to create an incongruity. The wilder the incongruity, the funnier we find the joke. An additional theoretical twist favored by some is that the incongruity should bring out an otherwise hidden similarity. So a general piece of advice for introducing humor to the classroom is to keep an eye out for the incongruous, especially connected with what you want to teach!

It is important, too, to recognize that jokes invariably have some anarchic tendencies built in. Each joke threatens to undermine categories or create unfamiliar worlds. George Orwell said that jokes are tiny revolutions.

CHAPTER SIX

Rhyme and Rhythm

Mickey Mouse's Underwear

This topic may need the least discussion, as most teachers are surely familiar with the various uses they can make of rhyme and rhythm in teaching literacy. Both rhyme and rhythm are by-products of oral language development; the purposes that drove the evolutionary development of language were aimed at uses other than these. They are solely incidental features of language development. But as with all humans' tool development, whether physical or cognitive, once something is available we begin to explore and exploit all the possible ways we can use it. People long ago discovered that the various sounds developed for communication could be shaped and patterned for greater impact and memorization and also for pleasure.

In teaching literacy we can help our students' exploration and exploitation of rhyme and rhythm to increase both the impact and the pleasure of literacy. These cognitive tools come along with oral language, and they are available, like the other cognitive tools discussed, to aid our students in learning literacy. Connecting this with Chapter 5's topic, one might encourage children to invent rhyming and rhythmic jokes based on common patterns, such as the "knock, knock" format. For reasons probably clear to any parent or teacher, typical four-year-olds fall around in hysterics at such old jokes as

"Knock, knock."
"Who's there?"
"Mickey Mouse's underwear."

The illogicality is overwhelmed by the fun of the rhyme and, to the four-year-old, the risqué content. Though, from the final words of the last chapter, we can see how incongruity is one of the mechanisms that makes the joke work for the average four-year-old. Children can be set in groups to invent their own variants, with varying degrees of direction and help given by the teacher.

Echo Rhymes

One of the teachers I worked with has children play with echo rhymes, which can be found everywhere in language, not just in verses. She shows how they are used for many purposes, sometimes for emphasis ("hurley-burley," "claptrap"), sometimes for humor ("boob tube," "drunk as a skunk"—one that usually is greeted with laughter), and commonly for abuse ("namby-pamby," "hoity-toity," "local yokel," "nitwit"). She asks students to find rhyming terms, using various categories—for emphasis, humor, abuse, and so on. So she writes a list of words, such as

fair

go

socks

past

wheels

fat

The students are invited to come up with rhymes. That set produced

fair and square

fair share

go with the flow

rocks in my socks

a blast from the past

meals on wheels

fat cat

and many more. After just a little of this, we discovered the students talking in such rhyme forms very easily and quite creatively.

One of the simpler uses for rhyme and rhythm is to help students remember principles of literacy. It was discovered by our ancestors long ago that any message coded into a rhythmic and rhyming form was much easier to remember than if those tools were not used in composing the message. This principle doesn't need to be restricted to slightly unhelpful rules like "'i' before 'e' except after 'c.'"

Rhyme and Rhythm: Ring, Rang, Rung

Nearly all literacy teachers use rhyme and rhythm to some degree. Most common perhaps are those exercises where the teacher provides a word and invites the students to say, or later write, rhyming words. One might write "pill" and give spaces for two or three words like "till," "spill," or "drill." Many use the common and useful practice of having students clap syllables and then play around with the emphasis given to the syllables by varying the pattern of clapping. (So Mar-ga-ret—clap, clap, clap—can be varied by a longer pause after the first clap or before the last.) Such exercises work on an important feature of language, but there are ways to extend the uses of rhyme and rhythm in the classroom.

Ms. Johal encourages her third-grade students to feel language and its rhythms as being tied closely to their body and its rhythms. She starts a small game with musical words like "sing, sang, sung" or "ring, rang, rung." Then she asks the students to place their thumbs and forefingers on their throats as they sound these words aloud. As they move from present "sing," to past "sang," and to past participle, "sung," the vowels follow the pattern back in the throat. As the students write the words, she asks them to reflect on the shortness of the vowel in the present tense, the longer vowel for the past, and the longest for the past participle.

Many of the routine exercises that deal with sight words and phrases can be enlivened by introducing elements of rhyme into them. Adding prefixes or suffixes, making plurals, using synonyms, and so on can all be done with rhyming terms and can often be made quite funny as a result.

Rhyme and Rhythm in Rounds

Rhythm not only is a movement of sounds in a phrase or sentence but also exists at the deepest levels of our consciousness. We develop a sense of the appropriate rhythms of expectation and satisfaction, hope and realization, fear and nemesis. These may derive from our earliest experiences of hunger and feeding, the beating of our hearts, and other natural regularities. For the everyday activities in the literacy class, we can draw on the patterns that have become established in our consciousnesses and those of our students. We might draw on the recognition of rhythm to support early word recognition tasks. The old practice of singing or chanting rounds can be adapted to engage each learner in repeating a sentence in overlapping turns. The ear can support the eye and vice versa. To take an old English example, which a number of our teachers tried with more success than anticipated, the teacher writes out the rhyme and points to the words as the children sing

London bridge is falling down,
Falling down,
Falling down,
London bridge is falling down,
My fair lady.

The first student, or group of students, begins when the teacher reaches the fourth line, and they chant that together, and then as they go on through the verse, the second group picks up when they reach the fourth line and so on. For rounds to work well, a little practice is required. But the rhythm is a strong one, and students soon learn the constantly repeated words. They have to recognize the pattern and attend to the words in order to know when to come in. Usually the community of rhythmic chanting is most enjoyable.

This particular example may be inappropriate for students in some countries, of course. But local examples will no doubt be available, and the teacher can adapt any popular rhythmic verse to a round.

Nursery Rhymes

Of universal appeal are nursery rhymes, such as the Mother Goose collections. They give delight; they introduce vocabulary; they make language "visible;" they introduce the pleasure of patterned speech; they introduce a sense of history and different times, places, and conventions; and they hint at deeper meanings below their surfaces and so introduce children to poetry and prepare them for more sophisticated poems.

Ring a ring o' roses,
A pocketful of posies.
Tisha! Tisha!
We all fall down.

Now there's a simple rhyme, cheerfully played out by generations of children, in many variations, that carries in it the folk memory of the Black Death of 700 years ago. And there is poignancy in odd rhymes, like: "There was an old woman / Lived under the hill; / And if she's not gone, / She lives there still." And what's going on in "Jack be nimble, Jack be quick, / Jack jump over the candlestick"? Or in: "Old Mother Goose, when she wanted to wander, / Would ride through the air on a very fine gander"? And "Here am I, little jumping Joan, / When nobody's with me I'm always alone." And what history is wrapped in: "Lucy Locket lost her pocket, / Kitty Fisher found it; / Nothing in it, nothing in it, / But the binding round it"? Who were Lucy and Kitty? Well, from some accounts, better not to ask. And what about "the little boy who lives down the lane," or, in some versions, "who cries down the lane," who is not going to get Baa Baa Black Sheep's wool? There he sits since our childhood, wool-less still, and for reasons we don't know. Such questions are not explicit in the child's mind, of course, but they are hidden echoes and stimuli to thought that come along with the rhymes, and they may detonate only years later.

Many books have suggestions about how rhyme and rhythm and early literacy development can ride along with music. Giving children a variety of small instruments—triangles, cymbals, shakers, drums, and so on—can enrich their experience of many nursery rhymes.

Children's own abilities to generate rhymes and rhythms can be developed on the back of nursery rhymes they already have learned. A simple activity might involve the teacher changing the first line of a known nursery rhyme and asking the children to suggest a new second line, such as this one that Ms. Eaton's class produced:

Humpty-Dumpty sat on a chair.
Humpty-Dumpty had a great scare.
All the king's horses,
And all the king's cows,
Couldn't get Humpty to come out of the house.

(In this case she also switched the last word of the fourth line.)

She then had the children work in groups, giving each group a varied first line to work with. One of the groups came up with

Moo, moo, black cow,
Have you any milk,
Yes, sir, yes sir,
Carried home in silk.

Another group produced "One, Two, / Buckle my belt; / Three, four, / How tight it felt." Another set had "One, two, / Buckle my lip;/ Three, four, / Can't eat a chip." Then there was "Jack be nimble, Jack be strong, / Jack go hit the dinner gong." Another was "Jack be nimble, Jack be bold, / Jack never did what he was told." And "Jack be nimble, Jack be clever, / Jack pull down the toilet lever." Oh well— the children produced many more and had a good time doing it.

They also enjoyed playing rhyme games with their own and others' names. This can be tricky, and the teacher needs to lead more than for some activities, particularly where it isn't easy to work out rhymes and rhythms for some names. After some examples for the whole class, small groups produced such forms as "Michael, Michael, Motorcycle." One group, in something like despair, came up with "David Lavid is a funny old Ravid." Ms. Eaton encouraged playing with the names, even daring to use an example that had dogged her from childhood "Isabelle necessary on a bicycle." It took a while for some children to understand that, but then it quickly led to such name play as: "Josh-u-are funny" and "Margar-ate it all," and many others. It was hard to conclude such sessions.

It is hard to think of any of the usual practical activities of literacy classes that cannot be enlivened by introducing rhyme and rhythm. Again, we don't want to use these readily accessible resources all the time, but recognizing that they are capacities already well developed by our students, it would be unwise not to draw on them with some frequency.

Teachers, Try It Out

1. Can you think of a technique based on rhyme and rhythm you might use to teach spelling?

2. How could rhyme and rhythm be used to teach the use of full stops and commas?

3. How might rhyme and rhythm be used to teach students to identify the main point of a short text?

Final Words

When children play with rhyme and rhythm they are sharing an activity that has given small but continuous pleasure to human beings from the beginnings of language use, everywhere in the world. No child now does it, but nearly all English-speaking children are familiar with "One, two / Buckle my shoe." These simple poems, in which sense is often a distant second to good, strong rhythms and clear, ringing rhymes, are foundational to a wide range of literate achievements. They introduce patterns of language and with them, possibilities of wit and much laughter. These are not gifts to ignore.

CHAPTER SEVEN

Living Knowledge

Barbie and The Matrix

This chapter heading is intended to emphasize a feature of knowledge that is widely recognized but which does not often influence teaching. We are all familiar with learning that is valuable because it enriches our understanding in ways that go beyond just the knowledge itself. Too often, however, we accumulate knowledge for the main purpose of passing examinations, after which it is commonly forgotten and never used again. This kind of inert knowledge—learned because we need it for some purpose extrinsic to our lifeworld and its engagements—was and is less common in oral cultures. In oral cultures, communication occurred very largely by means of the voice and the actual impact of the sound waves on the body of the hearer. In such circumstances, the emotion of the speaker, whether highly or little charged, always comes along with the words.

In literate cultures, of course, we pride ourselves on our ability to disengage our messages from our emotions. In fact, it requires great skill for us to reliably convey emotion through written words. You probably have no sense of the emotions I feel as I write. For all you can tell, I might be weeping miserably, tears dripping onto the paper, having already torrentially gummed up the computer keyboard, but I am able to hide all that by my choice of written words and the ability to revise them later. In an oral culture, the emotions could not be dissociated from the message.

The embedment of words in the lifeworld—the sense that our words are in some sense alive as parts of our body's activity—means that in oral cultures words do not become separated from things and activities. For example, oral cultures typically measure time in terms of communal activities. There are no clocks in oral cultures because everyone is attuned to the routine activities of the group, whether herding cows or digging roots. A meal might occur when the work is over or when a certain place is reached.

Once societies become literate, rational, and bigger, and people engage in separate activities, time needs to be measured in some "abstract" way, so activities can be coordinated. We do it by assigning arbitrary divisions and numbers to passing time and displaying them on clocks and watches, computers, video-recorders, microwave ovens, and so, inescapably, on.

Vygotsky's student, Luria (1976), described some of the studies he conducted with illiterate peasants in remote areas of the Soviet Union. Luria was interested in what seem to literate people simple logical tasks that the peasants could not perform. The syllogism he used with peasants is now quite famous: "In the far north all the bears are white. Novaya Zemla is in the far north. What color are the bears in Novaya Zemla?"

What became clear was that such logical games, wholly disembedded from the peasants' lifeworld, were completely unfamiliar to them. Quite reasonably, such tasks also seemed pointless to them. They politely told Luria that they had never been to Novaya Zemla, so they didn't know what color the bears were or even if there were bears. Why was he asking them such a question? He should ask people in Novaya Zemla or at least people who had visited there. The bears around here, anyway, are all brown or black. What to us is the simplest logical task presented real problems for them because they had not been influenced by the disembedding logic that comes along with literacy. It should be added that the clear results reported by Luria have been questioned by others since. While we may find that many nonliterate people don't have this total inability to deal with such tasks, it is clear that training in Western forms of literacy makes such tasks much easier for us.

Nonliterate people also have difficulty answering what to us are such simple questions that we can't imagine asking them. "What two words can you make from the word 'caretaker'?" "What smaller words can you find in the word 'catalogue'?"

You would think it very odd if I were to compliment you on your intellectual prowess in answering "care" and "taker" and "cat" and "log." Yet people in oral cultures typically cannot answer such questions because they do not "see" language the way literate people see it. Your sense of what constitutes language is very largely determined by the kind of material you are reading now. We literates have come to see language as being made up of letters, packed into words, organized in sentences, and chunked into paragraphs. But such an understanding is created by the form of writing we have developed. It is important to remember that nonliterate people do not see language this way. And that, of course, goes for our students no less than for people in oral cultures long ago.

The embedment of thought in the lifeworld is seemingly much more vivid and prevalent prior to literacy. Consequently, those whom we hope to make literate will likely retain greater or lesser degrees of this embedment of thought. As a result, we need to consider both how we might use this cognitive tool in our teaching of literacy and how we might ensure that we do not undermine it more than necessary in the process.

Embedding Knowledge in Students' Lifeworlds

The older style of literacy instruction that was driven by the perceived logic of the topic, rather than by the psychology of the learner, tended to ignore the student's lifeworld and experience. Or if the student's experience was not ignored, it was not seen it as an important factor in deciding the kinds of practical activities literacy learning should involve.

But while there has been general improvement in this area, it is not clear that the full implications of embedding knowledge in students' realities are recognized, especially if we look at various modern materials that are widely used to teach literacy. Again—to complicate the issue further—we must remember that many adults and children just beginning to learn how to read will have lived most or much of their lives in literate environments. With technologies such as TV and radio, not to mention video games and computers, most students receiving literacy instruction will already have picked up various forms of literate thought. But those forms of thought will not have been well supported, because the students will have had only marginal access to the literacy that supports them most adequately.

Emotionally Energetic Language

What *is* well supported, and perhaps better supported for non-literates than for literates, are the forms of thought and language use that are emotionally energetic. By this I mean the highly emotional ways in which people express themselves, which are typically banned in the classroom. In some cases, such talk with adult nonliterates will include rich and colorful profanity, in others a proficiency with vulgar gossip, and so on. Contact with literate environments can render such students inarticulate. Now this is not to suggest that all nonliterates have majestic gifts of oral articulacy which literacy destroys. Rather, we all know nonliterates who enjoy a fluency and vividness of expression, when socially unconstrained, that some of us high-literates envy. A language embedded in the user's lifeworld, as opposed to a seemingly remote academic subject, commonly has an energy and immediacy that literacy can suppress.

For some students, the most energetic of their oral language use may be evident only in their talking with siblings or friends. If that is so, then that language should be sanctioned as appropriate for *some* of the exercises of the classroom. If it is vulgar language, then that too, in some not-entirely-controlled form, must also be sanctioned for some activities. The delicacy comes in ensuring that this does not become offensive. It is of course so much easier, even if unconsciously, to apply rules of discourse in the classroom that effectively separate literacy from the most energetic language-use of the students. I am not suggesting that literacy teaching should take a radical turn by permitting bad language. Rather, by incorporating realistic aspects of students' lives, it is possible to develop the full and effective literacy achievement that is our aim.

Using Vivid Language in Teaching

How can we do this? For some adult students, exercises on plurals might use phrases like "Smash the damn window" or "The criminal stole the car" or other such sentences in contexts that the teacher feels might be safe. The teacher shouldn't, of course, insist that all students work with such sentences! For younger children who are fluent only in talking with their friends, exercises can draw on that form of language. Exercises in tense changes can use sentences like "Why does your aunt go to that shop so much?" or, more complex, "If you bring that doll, they won't let you in."

If the teacher prepares sentences that require the students to discriminate between homophones, for example, choose those that relate to the students' lifeworlds and their energetic language rather than the more dull cloze examples commonly used. Instead of (pair, pear) There is a _____ tree in her garden;

we might have

(toe, tow) The bullet shot his _____ off.

Now, you may be thinking that bullets aren't part of the average students' lifeworlds (at least, let's hope!). But keep in mind that students' worlds include their *imaginative* worlds, and for many students, shooting off toes is more familiar than pear trees and gardens. Of course, for some students, the ordinary examples might be as appropriate. But more engaging examples suggest to the students that even simple literacy exercises need not be about unfamiliar or, worse, boring words and language.

Children's Lifeworlds

How does the lifeworld of children differ from that of adults? In some cases, there may be little difference. The key is to ask what the children talk about when they are not in class. For young children, potty talk is often a much-delighting topic. Boogers and farts are much more engaging than trees and cats—though, of course, not for all students. Robert Munsch has a particularly wonderful story about a fart that comes to life in *Good Families Don't*. Getting ahold of your students' attention may be as simple as being up to date on the newest fad, be it Pokémon (now fading), Barbies (still!), or whatever—look in the local paper or chat to some kids. Whether teaching adults or children, the key is to remember that they have a rich lifeworld that may be quite different from the sanitized world of a typical classroom.

The Mystery Message

One common practice involves writing a "mystery message" on the chalkboard each morning before children come to school. The task for the children is to fill in missing letters, words, or punctuation. While the puzzle has its attraction regardless of the sentence on the board, interest picks up noticeably when more lifeworld topics are used. I'm not quite sure why, but the following sentence was a huge success with Mr. Ghosh's class:

"What's green and yellow and goes in a bun? A hot __og."

Mr. Ghosh had to keep pointing out that two letters were missing, until someone came up with the "f" and "r."

One of the more successful mystery messages followed a discussion of the "Matrix" movies with an adult class. The message read,

"_no_, I am ___ the chosen one."

It took some time for the students to recognize the need for a "K" and "w," and add the full word "not."

The general point of this chapter shouldn't be news to any literacy teacher, and nearly all books about literacy since the early twentieth century have tended to make some similar point. Given my frequent emphasis that we need *not* be constrained by students' daily experience and environments for our subject matter because we can also draw on their imaginative experience, it seemed wise to point out that this principle doesn't mean that we should ignore their daily experience and environments. Because there already exists such an emphasis on drawing on the students' immediate experiences and lifeworlds, there is no "Teachers, Try It Out" section for this chapter.

Conclusion to Part I

The cognitive tools discussed earlier, such as stories, metaphor, binary opposites, and so on, do not simply dissipate when initial literacy develops. They remain with us throughout our lives, perhaps changing form in response to our addition of increasingly sophisticated tools. It's certainly possible (and advised) to go through the list of oral tools again and think about how you might vary the exercises as literacy advances. As I have emphasized from the beginning, most students who attend literacy classes will most likely have lived in literate environments, and so the examples I have given earlier presuppose some literate thinking capacities. My purpose here is not to give an exhaustive set of exercises so much as to show, however generally, that this approach has direct practical implications.

Taken as a whole, the set of examples suggests a somewhat distinctive turn for literacy teaching. The most basic premise that follows from the previous chapters is that literacy teaching might be more effective, at the most basic level, if it is enlivened by more expansive educational aims. Utilitarian skills might not be best achieved by utilitarian methods; those skills might be best and most effectively achieved as incidentals to more imaginative educational aims.

What They Know or What They Can Imagine?

Everything we want children to learn about literacy was invented long ago for human purposes and is attached to human hopes, fears, and passions. One important task for teaching literacy is to recognize that the slow accumulation of detailed mastery of the tools of oral language connects with the deepest of human emotions. We won't expect to have those emotions dominating our classrooms each day, but we do need to recognize that literacy is tied into those emotions and that some connection should frequently be made to them. Once we lose any connection between the tool kit of literacy and the students' feelings, we reduce literacy learning to a crude acquisition of skills removed from what can give them life and meaning.

For the teacher struggling to achieve basic literacy with students, talking about feelings and rich meaning can seem unrealistic and beside the point; crude acquisition of skills would, in these circumstances, be an adequate triumph. But in reality, the basic task of achieving "crude" skills is actually made much easier if we engage the imagination and feelings of the students in their learning.

Part II

The Cognitive
Tool Kit of Literacy

CHAPTER EIGHT

Extremes

The Queueing Subbookkeeper

Apart of the folklore of education, as we saw earlier, is that the teacher should begin with what the students know and gradually build knowledge on that. I suggested that this principle, if taken in the literal way it is usually presented, can be and has been very damaging to education. If we include students' imaginations in "what they know," however, then we can expand the utility of the principle. If you flip through the *Guinness Book of World Records* (2002) or watch episodes (or read books) of *Ripley's Believe It or Not,* you find very odd material presented. Why should anyone care how many people can cram themselves into a small car, or who had the longest fingernails or beard, or who has jumped the farthest or lifted the heaviest weight? What has such information to do with the lives nearly all students lead? And yet we know that this kind of weird information is absorbed with enthusiasm by students the world over. They also love to read about terrible disasters, gruesome murders, babies born with two heads, and images of heroes that appear in blurry pictures taken over mountains or seen in decaying cheese or in water stains on walls. What's going on here? If the earnest advice is accurate that to engage students' interest we should begin with something that is a part of their everyday environment, then these kinds of fascinations shouldn't exist. But they do.

The Strange, Exotic, Different, and Wonderful

What seems to engage students' imaginations most readily isn't the everyday world around them so much as knowledge of what is strange, exotic, different, and wonderful. This doesn't mean that they can't also be engaged in their everyday world, but it does suggest, paradoxically, that we might better understand how to make the everyday engaging to their imaginations by considering what it is about such exotica that captures their minds. We cannot take it for granted that students are engaged by what they are familiar with or that they understand what is familiar. Focusing on the strange and wonderful might help us better understand how the local and familiar can be made interesting, rather than taking for granted that the familiar is a good foundation for new knowledge.

One simple observation that we might make is that when students are engaged by things in the *Guinness Book of World Records*, they may be interested in their everyday world. By learning who was the tallest and smallest person, or the hairiest or longest fingernailed, they are learning something about the context and the limits within which their real world exists. They are not so much leaving mythic thinking behind as learning a new kind of thinking and acquiring a set of cognitive tools that gives them a new purchase on reality. They are gaining security and confidence in dealing intellectually with a real world that earlier they had taken so much for granted that it wasn't an object of particular intellectual interest.

Fascinating Reality

There's no question that students today are captured by amazing stories, wonders, and weird facts. This does not mean that our literacy class is to be taken up teaching this range of weird facts and grotesque stories, but, rather, that the teacher can draw on such observations about what engages students in designing lessons and exercises. The next few chapters, as well as the Appendix, provide many examples for how to do this.

The teacher can constantly throw in simple questions that explore some of the limits, extremes, exotica, or records of written language. As students learn the difference between vowels and consonants and see how the two are distributed in words, teachers can ask "most" questions:

- What word has the most vowels together?
- What word has the most consonants together?
- What word has the most consonants with only a single vowel or the most vowels with only a single consonant?
- What word has the most double letters?

Of course, you'll need to find the answers to these questions to satisfy the curiosity of your students. You're likely to find them in a number of those "Play With Words" books. Here are some answers, before you start searching:

- Most vowels: *queueing* (Though some spoilsport dictionaries give it only as *queuing*, most, including the Oxford English Dictionary, allow both.) *Queue* is an odd word in that it would be pronounced the same even if you lopped off its last four letters one by one.
- Most consonants together: *latchstring*—not exactly an everyday word.
- Most consonants with only a single vowel: *strengths*.
- Most vowels with a single consonant: there are a number, though perhaps the most commonly used is *eerie*.
- Most double letters: *bookkeeper*.

Richard Lederer, from whom I've taken these examples, suggests that a bookkeeper's assistant could set a new record as a *subbookkeeper* (Lederer, 1989).

Metalinguistic Awareness

The examples just given may seem trivial, but they are mildly engaging to most people who become literate, because they set some limits to what is possible with English writing. They sufficiently distance students to a point where they can see language, in some sense, as an object, as a tool. Even odd items—like the words whose letters have the most continuous dots (Beijing, Fiji) or those made up of letter sounds (essay–SA; enemy–NME; expediency–XPDNC)—contribute to this process of externalizing language from our bodies and examining the means by which we perform this strange magic. We sometimes call its product *metalinguistic awareness*. It is useful to recognize that such a serious-sounding condition can be brought about in part by examining peculiar and quite accidental features of written language.

We can encourage this reflexive awareness of written language as an imprecise code for mapping sound by frequently asking students simple questions such as, "What other combination of letters can make the same sounds as 'ch'?" (This reinforces knowledge of the "ch" combination and both its common sounds, while also making a small game for the students.)

A more complex form of this kind of puzzle would use Bernard Shaw's example of the illogic of English spelling: "ghoti" is one way of writing what is more commonly written as *fish*—"gh" as in *enough*; "o" as in *women*; "ti" as in *nation*. Students might be invited to take any common word and invent an imaginative spelling for it. Some might think that such a game would run the danger of reinforcing bad spelling, but in nearly all cases the reverse would be found to be true.

Exploring Extremes

More generally the sense of reality comes from first exploring the extremes of the natural, social, and historical worlds within which we live. Exercises, then, might prove more engaging and meaningful if we occasionally use them to convey exotic information. A common writing assignment for more advanced students is to convert a text from one format to another. The following conveys a piece of information that might be found to be exotic and surprising to a person in the United States. It does so in a dialogue form; the assignment is to convert it into straight reportage:

Jean: "Do you know what state is named after Julius Caesar?"

Tom: "None of them."

Jean: "No. One is. I'll give you a clue. In 55 BCE Julius Caesar invaded Britain. After a summer of battles, he withdrew his army for the winter to some islands off the coast of Gaul—what we now call France."

Tom: "That's the clue?"

Jean: "Yes. The clue is the name of the islands. They were called 'Insulae Caesareae,' (*pronounced Kaizerieye*) or Caesar's Islands."

Tom: "Never heard of them."

Jean: "Yes, you have. On those islands a particular breed of cow was developed, which was also as a result named after Julius Caesar."

Tom: "A cow? I give up."

Jean:	"Well, over the centuries "Caesareae" changed from Caesareae to Caeseri to Chesery to Chersy to Jersey. So New Jersey is really New Caesar."
Tom:	"Wow. Is that true?"
Jean:	"Sure is."
Tom:	"Hey, my uncle lives in New Caesar. Bet he doesn't know it."
Jean:	"When did you last see a Caesar cow?"

More generally again, we could build many of the typically con-textless exercises on such information as found in the *Guinness Book of World Records* (2002) or other collections of the strange and extreme. We might usefully keep such texts on hand and draw on appropriate examples when designing exercises for students.

Wonder in the Classroom

An Adult Literacy Class

As emphasized earlier, an important task for the teacher is to try to bring out a sense of wonder with regard to the topic of the lesson—at least occasionally. While it takes some effort to find the wonder in everyday occurrences, the resulting student engagement is plenty of reward for the effort.

Ms. Pybus chose to evoke wonder about government with her adult literacy class, taking on the challenge of trying to expose what is wonderful about modern political organizations: their complexity, their reliance on so many people playing their parts, their vulner-ability to abuses, their distinctness from place to place, their shaping by history, their attempts to devise and administer laws, and so on.

The students were asked to begin by saying all the words or phrases they associated with government, and Ms. Pybus wrote them on the whiteboard: citizenship; political parties; voting; ballots; the rights of citizens; schools, roads, and hospitals; law courts and lawyers; individual dignity; upholding ideals; taxation; patriotism; and a number of other words. As the list increased, she drew atten-tion to the complexity of all these interacting features that in one way or another related to government. The very class, she pointed out, played a role in developing the citizenship of the students, as it was supported by government-directed tax money.

She then asked the students to generate a second list, made up of those things the students could think of that challenged the ideal of good government. After a short time, the students came up with such items as illegal activity, cheating on taxes, not voting, politicians who lie to get elected, the rich buying their way out of legal difficulties, inadequate schooling or health-care, corruption, cronyism, political apathy, and many others. For some reason, they seemed better able and more eager to make the second list than the first.

Students were then asked to choose one of the first set of terms or phrases and to write it on their own piece of paper. Next, they were asked to reflect on what would be missing from government activities without that item. They wrote their thoughts down in note form. One student who chose *school* noted, "not learn skills for many jobs," "not know country's past," "not fit into society." Another chose *voting* and noted, "no power in system," "no way to change leaders," "no rights."

Ms. Pybus then invited the students to share their ideas about the effects on government and citizenship if the system they lived in lacked the particular items each of them had chosen. In the discussion that followed, it quickly became clear that many of the items overlapped, and something of the complexity of the whole system became clear. The purpose was not to stimulate wonder at this great complexity in a manner that suggested it should be considered sacred and ideal, but that, even with its faults, it showed something of human ingenuity in building complicated social and political systems that can survive and function despite the endless challenges and weaknesses they involve.

The final part of the exercise involved the students making notes about what they thought were the most important features of government activity. Ms. Pybus then helped them work their notes into a paragraph or two that became a compact definition. Given the process and the emphasis on what is wonderful about government and the organization of modern states, those definitions each contained some element that encouraged the students to see some kind of wonder in this unlikely topic. Obviously, there are parts of the world in which this kind of exercise would be inappropriate, but the principle can be adapted to any political system with certain alterations.

A Literacy Exercise for Children

In developing children's literacy, we might focus on the complexity and variety in nature and the constant struggle for balance. Children could discuss the complexity of food webs and the impact that a minor change can have on the environment around it. We could begin by asking the class what they know about nature. The phrases and words could be recorded in a way similar to the methods listed for adults.

The students could then create a concept map to show the interconnectedness of nature and write words and phrases that show and describe the connections; for example, trees have leaves, leaves fall to ground, leaves rot, and rot makes food and new baby trees. Incidentally, concept maps can be a very interesting mix of indexes, symbols, and icons and may prove to be a useful exercise in understanding the arbitrariness of written language.

Teachers, Try It Out

1. Take three items from the *Guinness Book of World Records* (2002) and show how they could be used to construct engaging lessons in the use of capitalization and punctuation.

2. Choose an obviously false story from a sensational paper—aliens landed, monster sighted, etc.—and design a lesson in critical reading.

Final Words

A sense of wonder is a driver of learning. "I wonder . . ." is the starting point of much intellectual activity, and it has already engaged the imagination. It is a cognitive tool that we can bring to bear on anything in the world, and we can bring it to bear particularly on the amazing achievement of literacy and our individual exploration of it. So evoking the sense of wonder about the components of literacy we are working with should not seem an odd thing to do. Indeed, it might well be a starting point for much lesson planning. Later we see how we can routinely do this, using the planning frameworks built from this and other cognitive tools.

CHAPTER NINE

Everyday Heroes

Spiderman and the Comma

The collective version of reality that myths provide for many oral cultures has the enormous psychological value of creating comfort and security for those who believe them. We may feel confident in believing that the world is not a flat disk sitting on the back of vast elephant that stands on the back of an even vaster turtle. Things just aren't that way, our sense of reality insists.

The new sense of reality that is opened up by literacy doesn't provide much easy security. At eight years of age, the real world can seem vast and somewhat threatening. Reality just seems to go on forever, and a great deal of it makes little sense. The most common strategy we use to deal with this threat—the cognitive tool we develop—is to make an association with whatever seems best able to confidently deal with whatever we remain insecure about.

One child might connect with the strength, skill, and confidence of a sports hero, while another with the power, freedom, and wealth of a pop star. Consider who your heroes are, and this will tell you something about what you remain insecure about. For our students, though, the need for heroes is usually quite strong, even if the hero is a father, mother, or grandparent. In them they see the qualities of wisdom, courage, and good sense that are required to deal confidently with the complexities of the real world.

In a sense, it is not the parent, sports hero, or pop star that the student most profoundly associates with. Rather, the object of association is the heroic human quality that the hero embodies—the courage, good sense, wisdom, power, wealth, and so on. The crucial point for educational purposes is that these qualities can be found in anyone.

Heroizing Literacy Tasks

Here I am, taking it for granted that when I hit these keys on the computer, letters will appear on the lighted screen opposite my face. Most of our daily tasks become routine and taken for granted; it is a necessary procedure or else we would go nuts attending to every feature of our environments. But it is a process that can be an enemy of education. The educational trick is to bring sharply to the fore—to heroize—that which we want students to associate with and engage with imaginatively. So if I turn my attention to it, I can see the near-miracle of ingenuity involved in transferring particular electrical impulses into letters on the screen. It's a process I barely comprehend— except that I know it isn't magic. I can wonder at the cleverness and convenience of this literate act, and I can wonder about how far this electronic mode of dealing with words might shape our under-standing in ways we hardly glimpse yet at this early beginning of the digitized world.

The common associations that are made with those qualities we recognize as best able to overcome the threats of the everyday world, which sometimes seem to control us and hem us in, can be readily incorporated into students' practical engagement with literacy. From discussions with students, we can identify people or things that they see as heroic.

Heroes in the Classroom

Earlier, we explored the comma as a great historical hero whose invention caused more changes than were managed by all the usual array of leaders and conquerors who are thought of when we look at historical change. This might seem an odd way to look at history, but it makes a lot of sense to see some of the greatest transformations in our behavior and understanding, in our social arrangements and economic activities, in our political lives and our technological developments, as caused by these tiny squiggles that constitute literacy. The first hero in our literacy classes is the strange and potent set of skills that forms the objects of our daily lessons. Each time we begin a new topic, it is useful to remind students that these trivial skills, which may seem dreary to learn at times, have transformed the world and human consciousness and can also transform their world and consciousness.

Celebrating Literacy Heroes

Lessons conducted by our teachers were full of heroes. Students were encouraged to see literacy *itself* as one of humanity's most heroic achievements, and the great minds who invented the lowercase letter, the first word, and so on were celebrated throughout the year. Ms. Randolph, a first-grade teacher, invented an imaginary calendar for the year in which the class celebrated Alcuin, inventor of the lowercase letter; Wontalk, the inventor of the first word; Wudshud, inventor of the rhyme; and many others.

We had a small celebration on the birthday of each, and we spent some time using their special inventions and honoring them. Ms. Randolph had prepared baseball card stick-ons for the calendar, with a sketch of each literacy hero. She used historical figures when they were known but also created believable fictional figures when we didn't know the real inventor. Among the real heroes was the English monk Alcuin of York (735–804). Ms. Randolph supplied the class with details of his life, with most of the short text dedicated to his greatest invention, the lowercase letter, and why it was so eagerly welcomed by the literate community, along with the rules for its appropriate use. This led to a little confusion, as some of our students failed to understand that not everyone among their friends at other schools honored such great figures as Alcuin. But after a while, it began to seem that it was the others who were odd, taking such things for granted and not realizing that they were among the greatest of human achievements.

Literacy as a Hero

Humans lived for more than a hundred thousand years with oral language before the invention of writing. All that time, no one thought writing was possible. It took great genius to work out the system we now take for granted. The following exercise can give students a glimmer of its power.

Upper primary grade students can be asked to think of some imaginary event, set far away, or some unusual experience they have had. They can then be invited to write about it, in a manner that creates the clearest images possible. Then they can give their writing to another student to read, and so discover how the small squiggles on paper can generate new images in the minds of others. They can then discuss their shared images and discover how they are not the same. The students can then be invited to rewrite their account to avoid the misunderstandings of the first draft and then exchange it with someone different. And they might then talk about the images and go back to a third revision.

Throughout, the hero is the magic of literacy. This perception pervaded our classes at a general level, and students picked up the sense that they were learning something very special and powerful. But this use of heroizing also had many simpler uses in our classes.

From Sean Connery to Harry Potter

Ms. Pybus discovered early on that she shared—let's call it "an interest"—in Sean Connery with a number of her adult class students. She found that even the most routine exercises were more engaging when built around the doings of the movie star than if based on nonexistent people, such as the endless examples in workbooks. So when she prepared an exercise on recognizing the difference between "am," "is," and "are," for example, asking the students to write the appropriate word in the space provided, her list looked like this:

1. Sean Connery ___ over sixty years old.

2. I ___ a fan of Sean Connery's acting.

3. The writer of the James Bond stories said "Sean Connery ___ James Bond."

4. There ___ more than eight James Bond movies starring Sean Connery.

5. Sean Connery and Meryl Streep ___ to co-star in a new movie.

An appropriate children's hero might be chosen instead for younger students, such as Anne of Green Gables, Harry Potter, Harriet the Spy, Spiderman, or a well-known athlete. If we use a passage requiring the students to insert punctuation, we might choose a piece that recalls some stirring or heroic deed. The exercise remains the same, but the use of literacy for the student is changed. Perhaps the change is only slight, but nevertheless, dealing with such content adds an emotional satisfaction that is absent when the experience of text is always at best utilitarian and at worst emotionless. We could choose any heroic story or a newspaper article describing an event in which someone behaved heroically, exhibiting some admirable quality with which students could associate. The principle we might use in choosing such a text is to locate one that we ourselves find moving.

As you determine which texts to use in such exercises, remember that an important value of literacy is its power to link the student to distant times and places. You are not limited to choosing stories that students find familiar. By focusing on the heroic qualities rather than the events themselves, students can associate with them directly and often more powerfully than with more ordinary examples that rely on familiarity of environment to hold the students' interest.

Heroic Experiences

Let's say you're teaching beginning paragraph writing to a class of third graders. Encourage students to write about something they found stirring or heroic in their experience—perhaps something a grandparent or a friend did. Usually we begin with some practical detail of the student's daily life. Instead we might encourage them to reflect on the heroic action and write notes about the things they remember. These need not be sentences, but just reminder words, like

> Uncle John, broken leg—John skip, skip—fell in, got the puppy—the kid's puppy—dropped in river—fell in and got it—went under.

Then the student can be asked to organize the events in chronological sequence:

> Uncle John with broken leg—the kid had a puppy—the kid dropped the puppy and it fell in the river—the puppy went under the water—Uncle John hopped and skipped on his hurt leg—Uncle John jumped in the water and saved the puppy.

Then the student can write a draft of the paragraph, share it with a friend to edit it, and revise it. In the revision, he or she might be encouraged to elaborate on what made the action so heroic—some reference to Uncle John's pain and perhaps, in the end, some reference to the small boy's happiness. I have used a fairly routine example, in place of actual examples that would have a much higher emotional content.

The students could be encouraged to heroize themselves. Ms. Martin encouraged her fourth-grade students to bring in photographs of themselves or send pictures from home computers to ones they used in school. They were then asked to compose a headline for some heroic event that could be invented or described from reality for a newspaper account. The first part of the exercise, which caused most energetic work, asked the students to generate an alliterative headline that brought out a key aspect of the event to be described. "Marvelous Marcia muscles media" topped a picture of a student helping her dad carry an old TV set. "Donald the daring darling doesn't dare drop dishes" was for a similar domestic picture. "Cranky Kate consumes cookies" illustrated what you might expect. "Shoeless Sean saves sea" was a bit of a stretch for a picture of him loading a plastic bucket with water on the shore. The students were then invited to write an opening paragraph in which the heroic activity was put in a lively form.

Old Lessons in New Contexts

In order to use the tool of heroizing, many of our teachers made a small shift in context in teaching lessons they had often taught in the past. Ms. Brodkin began a lesson she taught regularly, about making clear descriptive statements using appropriate forms of capitalization and commonly used punctuation marks. The small change for drawing on the new notion of heroes involved inviting the students to design Web pages for their heroes. They had to locate a picture of the chosen person (which included, as well as the expected pop and sports stars, Einstein, Mother Teresa, Martin Luther King, Achilles [in Brad Pitt form], Sitting Bull, and a number of other surprises). The students then had to demonstrate the proper use of "," "!" and "?" in describing the main heroic characteristics of their heroes.

Teachers, Try It Out

1. Plan a lesson or two in which students design a set of cards of their heroes (like baseball or hockey cards with, for instance, Einstein's picture on the front, with a brief caption, and appropriate information about him on the back).This activity can be used to teach the proper and different uses of capital and

lowercase letters, commas, and exclamation points and how these might be used in a game the students might then play.

2. Plan a lesson in outline form that uses students' associations with heroes to teach how to sort and prioritize information.

3. How might you plan a lesson that encourages cooperation in sharing work and revising draft paragraphs using text about students' heroes?

Final Words

The students' more mundane heroes were also frequently drawn into our lessons, and their presence added a lot of energy and imaginative engagement to classes. Few exercises couldn't be made more interesting, and expanded in engaging ways, by introducing heroes. We had it both ways: at the macro level of literacy with our major hero and at the micro level of everyday exercises in which their more local heroes featured prominently. It enlivened planning for us, too, when we could introduce our heroes to the lessons. Ms. Pybus's routine examples were weirdly transformed, she reported, when she was able to import Sean Connery into them. Not all the students, of course, showed the same enthusiasm.

CHAPTER TEN

Human Contexts

John Montagu, The Earl of Sandwich

This might seem a slightly mysterious chapter heading, and so I'll begin by unwrapping it a bit. As explained earlier, all knowledge is a product of someone's emotional engagement with it; someone either invents it as a result of an emotional commitment or someone uses it in their work or play for enriching their lives. Everything we know or can know is tied in some way into the emotional lives of the discoverers, inventors, or users of that knowledge. To make knowledge meaningful to students so that they can readily *feel* its meaning, it needs to come wrapped in the emotions that can show its human importance.

Think back for a moment on your own education and when you learned about Herodotus, the father of history. He conceived of a *mega ergon* (great thing done) as the result of the heroic qualities of individuals and recorded the names of those people and their deeds so that they would not be eroded by the river of Time.

This characteristic also finds an analog in the lives of typical modern students when they become literate. They also make strong associations with their heroes, and they rehearse their heroic achievements in their minds because those accomplishments help them deal with a complex real world over which they have little control. Their heroes, as are all heroes, exemplify an unusual degree of some ordinary human quality the students also share. It may be strength, skill, power, confidence, outrageousness, wit, beauty, or whatever. And as I also mentioned earlier, it is crucial to recognize that it is not the particular heroes that are the primary object of the students' association but, rather, the unusual degree of whatever human qualities they represent. This means that *anything* can be made an object of students' association if we build into it the kinds of qualities we see in heroes. And that's a trick we explore here.

Knowledge in a Meaningful Context

The principle suggested at the beginning of the chapter is that all knowledge is human knowledge and that we should provide the human context of whatever we are teaching. Understandably, it's just not realistic for most teachers to create such contexts for every student exercise, but often we can locate a human perspective to add a dimension of meaning to learning many words or literacy skills.

Most languages have a number of words that were generated as a result of the quirks of some individual or the power of a story in which a character's behavior or fate led to a new word. Students might find it interesting to be told about John Montagu, when the word *sandwich* is used. It appears he was so addicted to gambling that he did not like to take a break even for meals. He had his servants bring him slices of meat between two pieces of bread. He didn't originate this form of meal, but Montagu—the Earl of Sandwich— demanded it so frequently and publicly that it took on his name. "I'll have a sandwich" might have become "I'll have a John Montagu."

All the words we use come from complex worlds of human activities, and just occasionally, it will enliven a lesson to evoke something of those past worlds. In English, everyone uses the word *money*, but not many know its origins. In ancient Rome, the goddess Juno (for whom the month June is named) was seen as the source of advice or warnings—in Latin, *moneta* (at least, this is the smart money guess about why the temple to Juno was so named). The temple of Juno Moneta (Juno who warns) in Rome also housed the mint where coins were made. In due course *moneta* came to be used for the mint, then the stamp from which coins were made, and then the coins themselves. So our word *money* comes from Juno's temple, where people once made coins. While this does not locate the word in the life of an individual, it does remove it from the arbitrariness that surrounds most of our words (to those not wild about etymology) and puts it into a meaningful context of human activities.

Teaching Concepts Using Word Origins

An etymological dictionary, or one of those books that gives a brief essay on the origins of certain words, can be a considerable help to the literacy teacher. Literacy, as is now widely recognized, is more effectively learned if the student becomes aware of words in a new sense, seeing them as objects worthy of attention in their own right.

Homonyms

Ms. Constantino wanted to teach her students distinct uses of homonyms, and she took the example of *pool* and some of its meanings:

a collection of water

putting objects together

the game played with cue and numbered balls.

She assumed—correctly as it turned out—that the distinction might become easier for the students to remember, and more interesting, if they learned that the second and third uses come from the French for "hen." How? She explained that in her native Corsica, as well as in other places in France, there was a cruel, medieval game that involved throwing things at a hen. The person who hit the hen won all the things thrown thus far—they might be coins or other things of value. The game was called *jeu de la poule* (the hen game: "hen" = *poule*). *Poule* came to mean that which was at stake in the game, and so the English term *pool* meant a "stake." A pool was thus the accumulation of the stakes. The game of pool took its name directly from this. She found, as no doubt any teacher would, that when students are introduced to word meanings this way, they remember them much better and use them more confidently. An "etymology a day" that ties a modern word into the human activity from which it is derived can make the class more engaging and gradually contribute to students' metalinguistic awareness.

Linking Language With Purpose

Humanizing knowledge of language, in one sense at least, has fortunately become more frequent in recent decades as exercises try to integrate the language being learned with the life and purposes of the learner. Many texts on literacy emphasize integration with students' lives. But we can take this principle much further by searching out the human meaning embedded in our literacy uses.

For example, after his fourth-grade students visited a zoo, Mr. Kirwin wanted to begin a poetry unit, encouraging the students to think differently about what they had seen, to push beyond the conventional. Recognizing the principle of human emotions and recognizing that one can project human emotions in anything, he chose the Vita Sackville-West's (1930) poem about the "greater cats," which the students had seen in slightly better conditions than the old-fashioned cages of the poem.

The greater cats with golden eyes
Stare out between the bars.
Deserts are there, and different skies,
And night with different stars.

They discussed why Sackville-West (1930) might see deserts and different skies and stars in their golden eyes. And why she came to see the animals' eyes similar to human eyes, filled with nostalgia for places long ago lost. The animals' stares were made meaningful only to the degree that they were imbued with human emotions. The author doesn't say that, of course, and the big cats' feelings and cognition are unknowable, but the resonance of the poem comes from our projecting onto the cheetah or leopard our feelings at being caged in an alien environment. Mr. Kirwin didn't use those big 32¢ words, of course, but those were the ideas he explored with the students, expanding their senses about what they had seen in the zoo. When the children were asked to write notes for a similar poem they might write about another animal they saw at the zoo, Mr. Kirwin said the results were much more interesting and deeper than those he had received in the past.

We spent a short time in one of Ms. Eaton's second-grade classes inventing a family called The Proofreaders. There was Momm and Daad Proofreader, and their two children Dawid and Kirstn. They described their job this way: "Wen peoples have writ something we read it again and make write all the rongs they have writ. Evryones shud do this al the time so there are no mistakes in the writin becos that's not polit." Unfortunately, they weren't the most successful people at their chosen job and in fact were treated rather shabbily by the professional group of Proofreaders. But they were really a very nice family and wanted to be as helpful as possible. The problem was that they were going to be expelled from the Proofreading profession if they didn't do their job a lot better. The class was enlisted to help them.

In future, whatever was written in the silent writing times in class would be given to the Proofreading family to check it out, but the class would be enlisted to make suggestions first. The class was fortunate in having a set of portable computers for writing and wireless connections so that files could be shared around easily. The children were first invited to help the family with their names and the description of their job, showing how they should carefully proofread what they had written and correct it, and helping their children David and Kirstin become better at the job than their parents had been. We played up the human quality of courtesy as basic to proofreading, and raised it, with a light hand, at frequent intervals. Mainly we emphasized how proofreading before "publishing" their scripts was a courtesy to their classmates and also to readers whom they would not know.

Teachers, Try It Out

1. How might you enrich the meaning of a short poem by setting it in the context of its author's life? Choose a poem and describe something about the author's life that would enable you to more richly teach about the poem.

2. How might you use the human quality of tenacity or of courage in teaching about some aspect of punctuation?

3. Design a lesson in which you encourage students to recognize forms of language shaped by different strong emotions—love, anger, fear, and so on.

Final Words

It is too easy to dehumanize the classroom by focusing on the skills we want students to acquire and forgetting the human qualities that they exemplify, that they are produced by, or that they serve. By constantly thinking of human contexts and the ways the skills find expression and meaning in human lives, we were able to make the classes more interesting to both teachers and students. Initially, some of the teachers found it a bit of a strain but quite quickly found it more natural and easy to think this way. If one looks at the material of literacy textbooks in terms of human qualities, a dimension of richer meaning is added that can help clarify what the exercises are all about. As in one of the examples, proofreading isn't just a set of skills, it's primarily a matter of courtesy. And recognizing it as such is to imbue the skills with human meaning.

CHAPTER ELEVEN

Collections and Hobbies

Alphabets and Beanie Babies

When engaged in workshops with teachers, I sometimes ask what they collected as children or teenagers. The variety of things is usually astonishing, certainly to the other workshop participants. People usually admit to such common collectables as comics, baseball or hockey cards, dolls, stamps or coins, books by a certain author, records by a certain singer, but also keys, maps, bottles, buttons, spoons, egg cups, and, in more cases than people might expect, items that are truly exotic. Often the teachers say that they still have their collections and even sometimes add to them. In most cases, though, the collection has been lost in a move, or given away, or abandoned in their early or mid-teens, or often they can't even recall what they did with it—maybe they threw it away. When I ask them why they collected such things, they usually describe an event, or a sibling, that got them started, but they have difficulty recalling the source of the enthusiasm they once had and often seem surprised when they are encouraged to remember just what their collections once meant to them.

What is going on? Why does nearly everyone collect something, at least for a time, or have a hobby that involves developing expert knowledge or skill about something very particular? I have tried to give an answer elsewhere (Egan, 1997), the crux of which is that with the onset of the sense of reality accompanying the growth of Western-style literacy, students commonly develop some insecurity. They know they are a part of some vast reality of which they know very little. It could be infinite, after all, in which case their lives may seem pretty insignificant. By collecting something or developing a hobby, the student can gain mastery over some part of reality and see that it isn't infinite and that they can know its limits. They can thus gain some security.

The collecting tool typically kicks in around age seven, reaches a peak at about eleven, and dies out around fifteen. Commercial interests that recognize and exploit this tool also recognize that it has an undercurrent that seeks a complete, exhaustive mastery of something. They commonly produce items that are limited in number but numerous, like Beanie Babies or baseball cards, and that have basic features in common but are varied in details. In theory, it is possible to complete the set. At least, the collector needs to know that the set *could* be completed. For example, you could collect a copy of all the postage stamps made between 1867 and 1876. Those dates might seem random—they *are* random—but a crucial feature of the use of the collecting or hobbies tool is that the object on which it is used can be almost anything.

Collecting Letters and Words

If the collecting and hobby tool can be attached to anything, from Beanie Babies to stones to commemorative spoons to chalks to you name it, why don't we try to attach some features of that tool to literacy? We need only to observe the features of collections and hobbies that attract students' attention and then make our presentation of literacy topics have similar features.

Collecting the Alphabet

In the beginning, when the alphabet was invented, each of the letters had small wings attached to it. The Greeks thought of words as "winged" because they traveled through the air like birds, settling in someone's ear. The inventor of the alphabet, or rather the person who adopted and adapted the alphabet invented by the Phoenicians, was Cadmus, according to legend. As the ancient Greek historian Herodotus put it,

> The Phoenicians who came with Cadmus . . . introduced into Greece, after their settlement in the country, a number of accomplishments, of which the most important was writing, an art till then, I think, unknown to the Greeks. At first they

used the same characters as all the other Phoenicians, but as time went on, and they changed their language, they also changed the shape of their letters. At that period most of the Greeks in the neighborhood were Ionians; they were taught these letters by the Phoenicians and adopted them, with a few alterations, for their own use, continuing to refer to them as the Phoenician characters—as was only right, as the Phoenicians had introduced them.

The Greeks, crucially, added vowels to the consonantal alphabet they learned from the Phoenicians and so constructed the system that we use today, with a few more changes to some letters introduced by the ancient Romans.

A comparison chart of Phoenician, Greek, and modern letters can take further the great story of literacy that we tell as a part of the process of our students' learning it. An animated graphic exposition of the changes is available at http://edsitement.neh.gov/Phoen_Greek_Anim.asp, and a detailed outline of a unit on this topic for five- to seven-year-olds can be found at http://edsitement .neh.gov/view_lesson_plan.asp?id=517. It is easy to make the mistake of thinking that a subject like the history of the alphabet is properly the realm of only advanced scholars. While learning their own alphabet, students can become fascinated with the set of letters and how they changed long ago into the forms we are now so familiar with. Don't be shy about having students learn the Greek and Phoenician alphabets. While few adults today can read any ancient Greek, learning things like this has never been known to hurt anyone, especially if it is part of the fascinating story of the development of literacy, which is the very adventure we are engaging students in.

So the alphabet itself can be the first set the students can collect, then they can learn its sources in earlier alphabets and also syllabaries and hieroglyphic forms of writing, and the changes it has gone through over time. The importance of the alphabet to human civilization can also be approached via the story of Cadmus sowing the land with the letters that became soldiers who enabled him to bring order and civilized life to ancient Greece.

Palindromes

Palindromes, words and phrases that are spelled the same backward and forward, are mild fun when first discovered:

"Madam, in Eden, I'm Adam."

"Ma is as selfless as I am."

"Live not on evil."

"Are we not drawn onward, we few, drawn onward to new era?"

It is an engaging challenge for students to try to come up with their own palindromes—and easier than might be expected, as long as we don't become too ambitious early on.

Literacy as a Hobby

Because we play with language all the time, and because it is so varied, it is a wonderful field for the collector or hobbyist. Teachers, for example, sometimes collect "howlers" from students' writing—mistakes that are also funny—and some have even published books of them or loaded them onto Web sites. Have you ever read student responses like these?

"The inhabitants of Egypt were called mummies. They lived in the Sarah Dessert and traveled by Camelot."

"Socrates died from an overdose of wedlock."

"During the Renaissance America began."

"The Pyramids are a range of mountains between France and Spain."

"Beethoven was so deaf he wrote loud music."

"H_2O is hot water, and CO_2 is cold water."

"Blood flows down one leg and up the other."

OK, OK, I'll stop—but I have had a good time doing this research. Well, all right, you might appreciate this final one: "Water is composed of two gins, Oxygin and Hydrogin. Oxygin is pure gin Hydrogin is gin and water." Of course, the kinds of howlers are more limited for the newly literate to collect, but students see and hear mistakes in language use every day. They could begin to keep a list of these, perhaps in the back of a notebook or in a computer file.

Related collections can be made of "found" or unintended meanings, some using common names, such as "Canada? [Can Ada?]" "I don't know, Alaska [I'll ask her]." "Emmanuel Kant but Genghis Khan." "There was no way, Zen there was." Other "found" expressions build on mistaken words: "Be alert; we need more lerts." Which is compounded by, "No, we have enough lerts. Be aloof." And can perhaps goes too far with, "No, no—be alert. There's safety in numbers."

Similar collections can be composed with a little research in the phone book or on the Internet, looking up people with oddly appropriate jobs. There really is, in Scotland, a Mr. Bones who is an undertaker, and in my hometown there's a singing teacher named Ms. Screech, and a Father O'Pray in New York (and the recently deceased Cardinal Sin of Manila), and there's a Massachusetts dentist named Dr. Fang.

Collecting Bloopers

Collecting bloopers in the press or in books can be a great stimulus to students' reading and careful attention to words:

"About one-third of all passengers flying between London and Paris travel by air."

"Not thrice but three times has lightening struck the barn on the Henry Summer farm."

"From 1800, until his retirement through ill health in 1928 . . ."

"Beethoven was handicapped by deadness."

"God was discovered in California in 1848."

Students could also keep a collection of graffiti, some of which can be very funny and some of which attempts to communicate serious messages. (I particularly liked one that read, "Don't cut hire education!") Or if the local supply of graffiti is not what you might want your students attending to, posters or signs could be alternatives. You could ask them to note what proportion of a poster was taken up with text and what proportion with a picture; what is the most prominent text; how many announce things for which the date has already passed; how many are political or religious or have to do with music or theatre; how many are advertising objects, and how many of each kind of object do they see posters for (cars, hair products, clothing), and what can be inferred from the relative proportions of each.

As may be inferred from some of the examples given, a popular collection might be a joke book. Computers allow students to easily find jokes on the Internet, and they can save those they find most engaging and add those they hear or make up themselves.

Students can also collect the kinds of words I have mentioned in other chapters—such as those with the most contiguous consonants or vowels, or repeated vowels but no other vowel ("defenselessness"), or the most sequential letters of the alphabet ("overstuffed" and "understudy" both have four letters—*rstu*—in consecutive order), and so on.

Codes

It is an easy step from such collections to what might become the hobby of codes. Students can be introduced to the simplest kinds of code, in which a message can be disguised.

J'n tvsf wpv bhsff.

By changing each letter to the next occurring letter in the alphabet, one can "code" the message "I'm sure you agree" in that mysterious seeming nonsense sentence. And why *are* the letters of the alphabet in that order? Coded messages are fun to compose, fun to decode when one has the key, and fun to try to decode without the key.

These games can also involve elaboration into the world of spying. The trick is to get information to the right people and prevent it from being understood by the wrong people. The "wrong" people can try to break the codes even though they don't have the key. Students might learn about the Rosetta stone as an introduction to their decoding attempts. Here are some other simple codes for students in Grades 3 to 5, which can be found at http://www.sciencenetlinks .com/lessons.cfm?DocID=284.

Example 1

Secret message: Hoouwtaordeayy?

Code type: Read every second letter.

How to decipher: Read every second letter starting at the first letter and, when you finish, start again on the letters you missed the first time.

Deciphered message: How are you today?

Example 2

Secret message: Sld ziv blf glwzb?

Code type: Reverse the alphabet.

How to decipher: A stands for Z, B stands for Y, C stands for X, and so on. To help solve this code, first write out the alphabet and then write out the alphabet in reverse below it:

A B C D E F G H I J K L M N O P Q R S T U V W X Y Z

Z Y X W V U T S R Q P O N M L K J I H G F E D C B A

Deciphered message: How are you today?

Example 3

Secret message: Woh era uoy yadot?

Code type: Reverse the words.

How to decipher: Read each word backwards.

Deciphered message: How are you today?

You can find a collection (!) of other codes at http://www.scouting .org.za/codes/

Teachers, Try It Out

1. How might you design a classroom in such a way as to engage all the students in a game of spies and codes so that certain people can read the codes and others must attempt to decode them?

2. What kind of collection would you recommend to help students not make mistakes in spelling commonly misspelled words?

3. Can you think of a game that would involve students collecting punctuation marks and learning their proper use?

Final Words

This has been a rather playful chapter, emphasizing the fun of collecting and hobbies, perhaps at the expense of their more serious aspects. Those more serious aspects connect with the sense of security I wrote about in the introduction. Mastering some area of knowledge can provide an important sense of security. While language is infinitely complex or may as well be, given our tiny grasp of its possibilities, certain parts of it are limited and can be mastered by anyone. Punctuation, for example, is made up of a limited set of squiggles and marks. Students can master all of them, even though in the process they will learn that there are no hard and fast rules about their use—except that their purpose is fundamentally one of courtesy between the writer and reader, making the written text more hospitable to the eye of the reader. This concept is elaborated on in the example about teaching the comma in Part III.

Writing is a code, and it can lead to many subcodes, which is why I have put more emphasis on learning to play coding and decoding games than is perhaps common in literacy classes. The attraction of the mysterious, of the secret, and the hint of spying all engage the typical student learning to master literacy. We would be wise to take advantage of this area of spontaneous engagement in our teaching.

CHAPTER TWELVE

Graphic Organizers

Lists and Flowcharts

We have seen that literacy in the ancient Mediterranean world was tied up with developing Western conceptions of reality. Literacy became a complex tool for trying to mirror reality, however problematic we might consider that ambition to have been (Rorty, 1979). But before that ancient Greek ambition took form, literacy had been used in a less complicated way to reflect what was real and true. Symbols were devised to indicate how many barrels of figs someone had for trade, how many cedar logs, or how much wine. By looking at such techniques found in the earliest examples of literacy, we can find clues about how we might make our teaching more appealing and useful to our students.

From the Ear to the Eye

Since 1919 a huge number of tablets have been excavated from the ancient port of Ugarit in Syria. Most were written around 1400 BCE. About two-thirds of the tablets are made up of lists—of taxes, rations, supplies, pay, inventories, receipts, census records, personal and geographical place names, purchases, loans, and so on. If we were to calculate the kinds of records sorted on computer disks at the moment, we might find that a similar proportion involves lists. The list is ever-present in our culture and has been one of the most common uses of literacy as well as one of the earliest.

89

Literacy is a process in which the eye begins to replace the ear as a major source of information. Perhaps that puts it too strongly, but clearly the eye becomes much more important. Equally as clear, the way the eye derives information from texts is different from the way the ear derives information from sounds. The process of early literacy instruction—if it is to be most effective—might, then, involve training in the techniques that make it easier for the eye to retrieve information. Now this is no simple matter, but let's focus on some simple, practical results.

Visual Tools

Lists

Once information could be stored in a written list, the mind was released from having to memorize items by tying them into memorable, rhyming, imagistic stories—so myths began to die away. In addition, the list remained available for visual inspection at any time and by anyone who could read. Once lists are recorded, they are open to, and often invite, reordering, categorization, and classification—and one need not fear that these manipulations might result in the loss of elements from memory.

Making and manipulating lists can have an important influence in achieving one fundamental aspect of literacy: the raising of questions, such as whether to classify a tomato as a fruit or a vegetable. This activity can help us to see one of the basic uses and values of literacy. The teacher might invite the students to write a list of fruits, for example, and then invite them to reorganize the list into those fruits with skins we eat, those with segmented insides, those with stones in the middle, those that grow on bushes, those that grow in "our" country, and those that grow in clusters. A list of sports may be broken into those in which a ball is kicked, those in which a ball is hit with something, those in which the goal is off the ground, those played indoors, those in which more than two teams compete, and those that can be played with only two people. Such simple illustrations indicate that the innocent-seeming list allows the learner to begin rational tasks that can show how literacy activities can enlarge our powers and, incidentally, provide some fun.

This activity can be performed on almost any topic. We could, of course, make lists for shopping and then divide those into edible things and nonedible things, and then divide these further into fruits, vegetables, dairy, meats, cleaners, paper goods, kitchen supplies, and so on. We could begin from a large undifferentiated box at the top of the page, then make arrows to two smaller boxes for the subcategories, then move down and make many smaller boxes for the basic categories. The utility of such list play for making supermarket shopping more efficient hardly needs discussion.

Flowcharts

The list is simply one of a set of literate tools that may enlarge students' capacities. A related one is the flowchart. This is simply a list organized by the principle of temporal sequence. It often has a direct and powerful utility. Practice in applying initial literacy skills to flowcharts can provide both straightforward vocabulary exercise and the satisfaction that always comes with mastery of a new and useful tool. Designing a flowchart of the student's daily activities and the main choice points faced during the day can be quite difficult, but engaging, to them. It is often surprising because the chart can lay out for the eye features of experience not before represented that way. Such a representation can provide a new sense of control over activities.

Rebus Signs

Another form of symbolic play that might exemplify this principle is the *rebus*. A rebus is a sign in which some symbols serve as words. The following worked well in Mr. Rodda's adult literacy class. Take, for example, the sign carried by a striking worker who thinks she deserves a higher salary:

I have to		paid
---------	because	----
work		I am

What is that supposed to mean? The first section says "I have to *over*work" and the second "I am *under*paid."

How would the students interpret this sign that appeared in a restaurant under the claim "Good value!":

<pre>
            M   E

            A   L
</pre>

Clearly the restaurant offered a square meal. Maybe students might have seen the following:

<pre>
                    0
                   BA
                   BSc
                   MD
                   MA
                   PhD
                   MSc
</pre>

—which, of course, means "six degrees below zero."
   Or how about

<pre>
                    B
       _____

        faults man quarrels wife faults
</pre>

This contains the sound advice to "Be above quarrels between man and wife. There are faults on both sides." (These examples have been adapted from Espy, 1982).

Other Visual Tools

There is a set of similar tools in which the eye's immediate access gives increasing control over features of reality. In our instruction, then, we will want to exploit uses of lists, flowcharts, diagrams, tables, databases, sociograms, recipes, and so on. In many of these tools of early literacy, events and processes and information can be routinely made available for reflection and action in new ways. Teachers who have not commonly used such tools might be surprised at how engaging most students find the simple activity of making and manipulating lists.

Teachers, Try It Out

1. Give an example of how you might use a flowchart to clarify for students the main indicators of tenses and moods.

2. Design a rebus for some common expression or proverb.

3. How would you teach a lesson that focused on listing the names of vegetables, and how would you subdivide the lists?

Final Words

In several places, this book has emphasized the importance of seeing language as an object for becoming increasingly literate. In this chapter the focus has been on seeing writing in forms different from those in which we conventionally see it. Being able to derive meaning from written language by using our vision is, of course, one of the distinguishing features of literacy. The point is that this central purpose can be helped along if we make ourselves aware of it and think about some deliberate ways of efficiently, and entertainingly, engaging our students in recognizing the utility of these early tools of literacy.

Conclusion to Part II

While the set of cognitive tools described in Part II is separated into distinct chapters for purposes of clarifying the natures and uses of the various tools, it is clear that they have common themes. These tools are like the different heads that can fit into a screwdriver handle—in a sense it's the same tool, but the subtool allows it to do somewhat different work. Not the best analogy perhaps, but it does get at why such themes as humanizing the curriculum content we are going to teach occur in each chapter, in one form or another. We have to look at each tool for its human core and the human characteristics that can give it life and meaning for students.

The other common theme of many of the tools is the sense of wonder. To us, especially if we have been teaching literacy for decades, it is often difficult to stand back and constantly remind ourselves how extraordinary an achievement the invention of literacy was. And even while we know it, capturing the wonderfulness again and again is very difficult. And yet, to teach literacy well, we do have to communicate this sense of wonder about what the students are learning, and the extraordinary adventure it has involved us in as a species and can involve each of us in as individuals.

The chapters in Part II provide some help, I hope, about how to humanize the features of literacy. To retain a sense of wonder about the subject, it may help to reflect on the strange history of literacy. Also, reflecting on the vast effects it has had on human societies and our everyday lives, on our very sense of ourselves, and on our power to know other minds in distant places and times can help. No other animal knows its great-grandparents, yet we know the intimate thoughts of people who lived and died thousands of years ago. It is by trying frequently to recall the wonder in this that we might be able to carry our students beyond the uses of literacy for simple utility and superficial entertainment.

Literacy is magic, and somehow the teacher's job is to take students to its utility and to its means for easy entertainment while showing that it has also been developed into something magical. Some define magic as being equivalent to technology we cannot understand. We use the technology of literacy, and we can teach it to others, but it remains a technology we will understand only when we understand all the recesses of the mind—and that seems a long way off.

Part III

Planning Frameworks

CHAPTER THIRTEEN

Framework 1

In the previous chapters, the cognitive tools that come along with oral language and with early literacy have been explored, and we have looked at how each tool might be used in teaching. In this chapter, many of the tools are brought together to build planning frameworks. These frameworks will enable you to build lessons and units that put engaging students' imaginations in learning to the fore.

To recap, in most teacher education programs, planning is taught in terms of the old model of first deciding objectives for the lesson or unit, then organizing the content to be taught, then planning the methods of instruction that will be used, and finally choosing the evaluation procedures that will tell us whether, or to what degree, the objectives we started with have been achieved. This has proven an important model for helping new teachers get a measure of control over the tasks of planning and teaching.

This Part presents a couple of alternative models, both of which should offer the teacher at least as much control and, in addition, engage the students' imaginations in learning. One model is designed for use with preliterate students and the other for students who are making some progress as early fluent readers and writers.

Each of the frameworks is made up of a set of questions about the topic to be taught. Answering the questions should provide us with a plan for the lesson or unit that should direct us to teach it so that it engages students' imaginations. Following the questions is some brief guidance about how to answer them as well as spaces in which to write your answers. You might find it useful to photocopy these pages for trying out the frameworks in planning various topics. After laying out the frameworks, you'll find examples that apply them to literacy topics. The previous chapters should help you answer the frameworks' questions successfully.

Some teachers who have had experience with these frameworks have found themselves mixing and matching elements from each. That can make sense in many circumstances, but let's begin by treating them as two distinct frameworks. See whether you think they may be able to add something to your planning and teaching. I start with what I've called the "mythic" planning framework. I have called it mythic because the most potent features of language use in oral cultures can be most clearly seen in the myth stories found in such cultures around the world. They use story forms and vivid images, rhyme and rhythm are common, binary oppositions play a large role, they move on metaphoric connections, and so on.

Mythic Planning Framework

1. LOCATING WONDER

What is emotionally engaging about this topic?

How can it evoke wonder?

Why should the topic matter to us?

In order to help students connect emotionally to the material, teachers first need to identify their own emotional attachment to it. A sense of wonder about something is usually connected to this attachment. Everything that we teach can evoke some kind of wonder and produce some emotional response in us and both are also important in engaging students' imaginations.

So this first question asks the teacher to *feel* for what is wonderful about the topic. This can be difficult if the topic is something like the use of the comma. The trick is to re-see the topic through the eyes of the students, to get at what can stimulate the sense of wonder about even the most routine topics. When teachers have been taught to become expert at organizing classroom activities and structuring topics into instructional units, this can be especially difficult. It is asking the teacher to do something that is, for most, quite unfamiliar—to begin by *feeling* about the topic.

Sources of wonder:

Sources of emotional engagement:

2. Thinking About the Content in Story Form

Finding Binary Opposites

What binary concepts best capture the wonder and emotion of the topic?

Now to the work of locating the best binary oppositions on which we can construct the "story" we are going to tell. It should be possible to select the one that seems best, though you might want to note some alternatives, in case you find the first set doesn't quite carry you through the lesson or unit as well as you expected.

> **Opposites**
>
> **Main opposition:**   _____ – _____
>
> **Possible alternative:**   _____ – _____

Finding Images and Drama

What parts of the topic most dramatically embody the binary concepts?

What image best captures the dramatic contrast?

Here the goal is to identify the drama inherent in the topic. Remember, every topic has some kind of dramatic conflict in it. What binary-opposite concepts best capture that conflict? Again, for you, as the teacher, trying to *feel* the drama is as important as thinking about it. This task, too, can be quite difficult at first. It does become easier as we begin to recognize that there is something quite usual about thinking in these terms. The drama of commas may not be so obvious nor how you might break up your lessons about commas into binary opposites. But everything has within it something dramatic, and as we'll see, everything can be broken down into binary opposites. We are so accustomed to thinking about content and about concepts that we often forget that every topic also has a wide range of images attached to it. And remember, the image can carry the emotional meaning of the topic and can also make it much more memorable—if we find a good image, of course. Look for a core conflict, contradiction, or drama that seems to best convey the wonder and emotion of the topic.

```
Image that captures binary oppositions:



Content that reflects binary oppositions:
```

Structuring the Body of the Lesson or Unit

How do we teach the content in story form?

Having done the hard work that has put in place the basic structuring elements—the binary opposites and the basic drama—it should be relatively easy to create a narrative plot line of the content. The opposites provide the cognitive and emotional framework of the story. Remember, all good fictional stories are built on a conflict or puzzle; the only difference here is that the "story" content is the curriculum content. It might help to think about the plot of the unit's story in terms of beginning, complication, and resolution.

```
Sketch of overall story structure of the lesson or unit:
```

3. CONCLUSION

How does the story end?

How do we resolve the conflict set up between the binary opposites?

How much do we explain to the students about the binary oppositions?

Every story has an ending in which the conflict is resolved in some way or at least explained. For younger students, a simple resolution may be appropriate; for older students, an exploration of the opposites and the dramatic space between them can be explored. The conclusion can therefore take on many forms: from students' presentations, to displays, to a story that shows another form of the opposition being worked out, to dramatic presentations of the story with visuals, and so on. Remember, the conclusion is another opportunity for students to feel the drama of the story and internalize the material while expressing their understanding of it in imaginative ways.

Concluding activity:

4. EVALUATION

How can we know whether the topic has been understood, its importance grasped, and the content learned?

Any of the traditional forms of evaluation can be used, but in addition, teachers might want to get some measure of how far the students' imaginations have been engaged by the topic. Various kinds of information, including that derived from discussion, debate, art work, journal writing, and so on, can be gained as the unit is being taught. The teacher can also measure the amount of nonrequired reading students engage in. They might also record what other reading or video watching they may have performed related to the subject matter. In addition they could ask the students to keep personal notes in which they record in an open-ended way any ideas they have had about the topic they are studying.

Example: A Lesson on Homonyms

Instead of beginning with objectives, this framework guides us to think instead of the importance of the topic, in particular to "perfink" (perceive, feel, and think, together) what is emotionally important about it. The main structuring device then follows. We are asked to reflect on which binary opposites catch that importance. This method works just like any story form: In the beginning the author sets up opposite forces whose interplay provides the organizing structure for the work. The binary oppositions also will determine for us what is relevant and what irrelevant to include in our lesson. We are then given some guidance in how to think of our lesson or unit as a story: We are to think of our lesson not so much as a matter of attaining objectives but as a good story that we are to tell our students.

This approach can have a significant influence on how teachers approach their task. They are to tell the great story of literacy and introduce students to its wonders. I know the daily business of classes can erode the ideal suggested here, but to have a planning framework that encourages such an approach seems only for the good. Literacy *is* a great story—the sheer cleverness of its invention and developments in the ancient world, what it has made possible for human beings, and how it has transformed our lives, both the internal life of our minds and the external lives we lead among the products of our sciences and technologies. To think of oneself as the teller of this intricate narrative is a step up from thinking of oneself as the facilitator of students' acquisition of sets of utilitarian subskills.

Mind you, one would want to be sure that telling this great story of literacy also ensures that our students learn the necessary skills better than they otherwise would. The conclusion asked for here is, again, an emotional one—a satisfaction of the opposition set up at the beginning. Also such a framework and its products should not be free from evaluation. In this case the evaluation might also include the emotional element. That is, one will not only test that students have mastered the material but one will also try to assess the degree to which they also are gaining some emotional understanding of the importance of literacy.

1. Locating Wonder

What is emotionally engaging about homonyms?

How can they evoke wonder?

Why should homonyms matter to us?

So what is the wonderful story about homonyms, those words that sound the same but have different meanings? What might we want to teach in a single lesson? Homonyms tell us something about the slapdash manner in which our language has grown. Our language isn't some neatly designed logical device but, rather, has all kinds of oddities that have served complex purposes. Or perhaps these oddities in our language were simply convenient, and there are only a limited set of sounds we can easily make. So we want to show homonyms as exposing some of the messiness of language but also showing the ingenuity with which we turn such messiness into wonderful results. To take one of the lighter topics mentioned earlier, let us assume that we want to have students recognize those two qualities of homonyms and decide to use the joke as the medium for conveying the message.

The joke remains primarily an oral form, despite books of them. Certain jokes pass from generation to generation, surviving sometimes with only superficial changes through decades and even centuries.

Jokes work by making a metaphoric connection between things otherwise not connected. The more weird or unexpected the connection or the more a joke asserts a logic that is thinkable but absurd, the more likely we are to respond with an explosive laugh. The laugh seems a result of our holding, for a moment, categories or images that suggest a world working quite differently from the way reality works. This applies at least to certain kinds of jokes, those that create deliberate confusion, usually by insisting on the wrong interpretation of a homonym. In their simplest form they can appear as those question-and-answer jokes: "When is a door not a door?" "When it's ajar."

Playing with such jokes encourages flexibility in the use of metaphor, introduces logic, can give us practice with the composition of narratives, and helps students understand what homonyms are and what problems they can cause and what benefits they can have for our language uses.

2. THINKING ABOUT THE CONTENT IN STORY FORM

Finding Binary Opposites

*What binary concepts best capture the wonder
and emotion of the topic?*

A useful structuring pair might be normal–weird. At the heart of many jokes is the contrast between what things go together in our expectations and what things don't and the sudden intrusion of something that does not fit yet makes a kind of sense. It is a kind of sense that shakes up the categories of our expectations. The incongruity often serves to reassert the normal course of events by its craziness, but in the moment of the joke it creates a wild, new, different world.

> ## Opposites
>
> **Main opposition:** normal–crazy
>
>
> **Possible alternative:** logical–absurd

Finding Images and Drama

What parts of the topic most dramatically embody the binary concepts?

What image best captures the dramatic contrast?

Take any homonym and think of deliberately using it incorrectly so that a crazy image is generated.

Image that captures binary oppositions:

An elephant leaving home, packing his trunk ("nose") full of clothes.

Content that reflects binary oppositions:

Nearly all homonyms can be twisted from normal use to something crazy.

Structuring the Body of the Lesson or Unit

How do we teach the content in story form?

The first part of this section invites us to think of a dramatic embodiment of the binary opposites that catch the importance of the topic. One way of getting at this might be to begin with a set of simple jokes. Here's a popular joke form in North America:

He: "Do you like my company?"
She: "I don't know. What company do you work for?"

"How do you stop a herd of cows from charging?"
"Take away their credit cards."

"How did the elephant feel about packing its trunk?"
"It sucks."

The teacher might begin with a brief analysis of these. The first is a case of deliberate misunderstanding of a homonym. The second and third also get some of their humor from being parodies of joke forms as well as using the form they parody. The third is based on a double incongruity; the normal act the elephant makes to fill its trunk is the sucking that can also be a comment on the elephant's feelings about the act.

This analysis should be quite brief. The teacher might then take the jokes further by asking the students, perhaps in groups, to take their favorite joke and continue the narrative. The teacher might prepare a few examples. Perhaps, if the teacher feels ready to be a little daring that day, he or she might, in an assumed voice, elaborate a crazy world from the confused homonym. In a TV-commentator-style of high seriousness, the teacher could continue the story of the last example with something like this:

> After the elephant had packed its trunk, I offered to take it to the station. But we were early, so I decided to take it home with me. Fortunately I drive a convertible car. Unfortunately, as we came to the driveway to our house, the elephant sneezed and shot the contents of its trunk all over the place. There were clothes hanging from bushes and trees and spread all over the lawn. I discovered then that the elephant was a girl, as a pink dress hung down over the bedroom window. A pair of red, polka-dot shorts was hanging from the aerial of our TV satellite dish, and a huge T-shirt was draped across the front door. Just then my wife opened the front door and said . . .

The teacher might invite the students to supply the wife's response and the next step in the zany narrative. The lesson might continue by getting the students to write or make notes about their favorite homonym-based jokes, possibly in groups. Each group might choose one to tell the class.

Such a class would involve some reflection on language, a study of how certain forms of homonyms can be used deliberately to cause the kind of incongruity that results in laughter, and some practice making notes and working these notes toward a coherent narrative. The exploration of impossible worlds created by taking a homonym crazily rather than normally can also help to underscore differences between written and spoken language.

---

3. CONCLUSION

How does the story end?

How do we resolve the conflict set up between the binary opposites?

How much do we explain to the students about the binary opposites?

A concluding activity might take a homonym at random and get students to invent a joke, based on the deliberate confusion of it. Take, for example, *channel*, as in narrow passages of water and as in TV. The task is to invent a question whose answer is wildly incongruous but coherent in the metaphoric slippage between meanings of the homonym. Immediately, students will suggest confusions between "crossing the channel" in a boat or on TV. Or questions such as "What [TV] channel is the wettest?" or "What [sea] channel is full of news?" will emerge. After some examples, the teacher can again extend the mad world that is created by deliberately taking the incongruous meaning literally and invite the students to elaborate it further. Some preparation time with the British TV show *Monty Python's Flying Circus* might help.

4. EVALUATION

How can we know whether the topic has been understood, its importance grasped, and the content learned?

The amount of laughter generated might form a unique evaluation instrument to such a lesson. The degree of engagement should also provide an index of emotional success. But we also want to evaluate how adequately students have grasped the role and uses of homonyms and the metaphoric slippage that can frequently occur among these features of language. Students' comprehension can be assessed by the adequacy of their explanations of how some of these jokes work. We could give them exercises that would require them to display how adequately they understand which words in a joke are the homonyms and how adequately they can explain how the homonym works. The jokes students create make excellent additions to portfolios.

Forms of evaluation to be used:

Observation of students' engagement and understanding of the topic as the lesson goes forward.

Assessment of how adequately they can identify what a homonym is and how adequately they can use the potential homonyms provided for humor.

CHAPTER FOURTEEN

Framework 2

Here is a framework that is derived from the second set of cognitive tools, those that were explored in Part II. It has in common with the first framework a beginning that seeks less for an objective and more for an important meaning around which the content of the lesson can be structured. There is a greater emphasis on how to tell a good story than on how to attain an objective—while using the good story as a better way of attaining that objective.

Both of these frameworks ask teachers to begin planning by reflecting on the importance they themselves can identify in their own lives and experiences. This needn't be some heavy-duty self-interrogation but, rather, a moment of reflection on something about the topic that can emotionally engage them, even in a small way. Implicit in such an approach is the assumption introduced earlier in the book that teaching is likely to be more successful if teachers have located some emotional response to the topic within themselves. Imaginations are engaged by something when some emotional tie to it is identified. Engaging the students' imaginations will likely happen more easily through showing them the emotional importance of the topic.

The Romantic Planning Framework

1. IDENTIFYING HEROIC QUALITIES

What heroic human qualities are central to the topic?

What emotional images do they evoke?

What within the topic can best evoke wonder?

What heroic human quality or emotion—courage, compassion, tenacity, fear, hope, loathing, delight, or whatever—can we identify in the topic? These "romantic" qualities help us—and our students—see the world in human terms and give human meaning to events, facts, and ideas in all disciplines. "Romance" invites us to view the world in human terms, not to confuse but to infuse the world with human meaning. Again, this first task is the most difficult part of planning the lesson or unit. We are asked to *feel* about the topic as well as to think about it.

Identifying Transcendent Qualities

1. Main heroic quality:

2. Alternative(s):

Images that capture the heroic quality:

---

2. Organizing the Topic Into a Narrative Structure

Initial Access

What aspect of the topic best embodies the heroic qualities identified as central to the topic?

Does this expose some extreme of experience or limit of reality?

For the first lesson of a unit or the opening part of a single lesson, teachers are asked to search their own imaginations for images that catch the heroic quality that can provide the dramatic structure for the unit. Remember, it is as important to *feel* the heroic qualities as to *think* about them. Rather than focus exclusively on the content and how it will be organized, teachers should also search their understanding of the topic and its content for those images that best capture what is important about it.

Exotic or extreme content that best embodies the main heroic quality:

Composing the Body of the Lesson or Unit

How do we organize the material into a story to best illustrate the heroic qualities? Sketch the story, ensuring that the qualities will be made clear by the narrative.

The principal heroic quality should provide the drama and conflict in the story. Remember, the qualities should be those that most effectively convey the content of the topic. In making this brief initial sketch, try to capture just the main narrative thread that will carry the students' understanding from the beginning to the end of the lesson or unit.

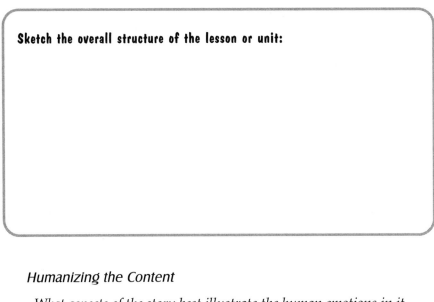

Sketch the overall structure of the lesson or unit:

Humanizing the Content

What aspects of the story best illustrate the human emotions in it and evoke a sense of wonder?

Think of how a good movie or novel makes aspects of the world engaging. Obstacles to the hero are humanized in one form or another, even possibly given motives; they are seen in human terms. To do this, there's no need to falsify anything, but rather, highlight a particular way of seeing it—because this is precisely the way students' imaginations are engaged by knowledge.

What content can be best shown in terms of hopes, fears, intentions or other emotions?

Pursuing Details

What parts of the topic can the students best explore in exhaustive detail?

While it is easy to give students a project to do, it is a little harder to think about what aspect of the topic they might be able to *exhaust*, to find out nearly everything that is known about it. But there are such parts in every topic, and the security and sense of mastery that comes from knowing nearly as much as anyone about something is a great stimulus to inquiry. Think of something that is intriguing, that can be seen from a variety of different perspectives, or that is alluded to but not examined in detail in the content or in your teaching of it (referring to your just-jotted notes should help).

List those aspects of the topic that students can explore exhaustively:

---

3. CONCLUSION

How can the topic best be brought to satisfactory closure?

How can the student feel this satisfaction?

We should end a topic in a "romantic" way, which can have two forms. The first form is to reexamine the images we started from and review the content through the lenses of other heroic qualities, including some that might give an opposite or conflicting image to that of our earlier choice. For a very general example, if we have all along been looking at literacy as the heroic maker of the modern world, then we might pause to consider how it also was involved in the destruction of the hunter-gatherer societies that preceded our literate world. The second form is to show how the romantic association the students have formed can help them understand other topics in a new, more imaginative, way. We can use both, of course.

Concluding activities:

4. EVALUATION

How can we know that the content has been learned and understood and has engaged and stimulated students' imaginations?

Any of the traditional forms of evaluation can be used, but in addition, teachers might want to get some measure of how much students' imaginations have been engaged by the topic, to what extent they have successfully made a romantic engagement with the material. In addition, the concluding activities are also evaluative in nature. Various kinds of information, including that derived from discussion, debate, art work, journal writing, and so on, can be gained as the unit is being taught. The teacher can also measure the amount of non-required reading students did. The students might also record what other reading or video watching they may have performed related to the subject matter. In addition teachers could ask the students to keep personal notes in which they record in an open-ended way any ideas they have had about the topic.

Forms of evaluation to be used:

Example: A Lesson on the Comma

I have used teaching about the comma as a shorthand reference to topics that can often seem most difficult to make interesting and imaginatively engaging, but I have also said that anything can be made heroic. So it's time to put my money where my mouth is. How can we make the comma imaginatively engaging, romantic, heroic, and all those other fancy terms I have been using?

Here is a unit worked out with Ms. Lopez for a Grade 5 class in her multiethnic school and taught by her. One of Ms. Lopez's virtues, it seems to me, is her recognition that students' imaginations are engaged by the richness of the content itself—they are not to be hooked by some neat idea and then have the material taught in traditional ways. The hook for her is the same as for this approach in general: the wonder inherent in the material itself. Her aim is to enlarge her children's understanding by making sure they understand the content of the curriculum. She is known as a teacher dedicated to making sure her students learn the specified material, and she has what many consider remarkable success.

Her success is partly due to her assuming that the imaginations of all her children, despite the variety of ethnic backgrounds and not a few of them dysfunctional, can be engaged by such content as the comma. With the best of intentions, many teachers in her school see the primary need of many of these children as social and emotional support, and they consider such things as comma use to be largely irrelevant to their needs. Yet it is the hard-nosed Ms. Lopez, who very deliberately emphasizes the content, who seems to be most valued by these kids. They see her as having faith in them simply because she clearly thinks they can learn well such features of good literacy practice as the proper uses of the comma.

1. IDENTIFYING HEROIC QUALITIES

What heroic human qualities are central to the topic?

What emotional images do they evoke?

What within the topic can best evoke wonder?

The framework directs us first to identify heroic qualities, affective images, something wonderful, something heroic about the comma. That might seem quite a challenge, particularly to those of us who were taught punctuation by traditional methods in school. I suggested earlier that one could introduce such a topic by putting it into the wider context of the historical story of writing's development. This is the approach Ms. Lopez took, believing that historical backgrounds are often a good way of humanizing topics that look purely technical. Someone invented the comma, after all, and had a reason for doing so and had hopes and fears like the rest of us. Our task is to see how the comma can be fitted within this human network of emotions, hopes and fears. It may be that we can't find the original inventor, but we can find the reasons the comma was invented and see it through the eyes, purposes, and emotions of those unknown inventors.

In early texts there was no punctuation, just letters one after another filling all the space on a page, tablet, or stone. Reading was difficult and, to make sense of a text, one would most commonly read it aloud. Punctuation is made up of a set of simple, elegant, and ingenious inventions that have been added to texts to make them easier to read. The heroic quality we settled on, then, was this simple, elegant, ingenious inventiveness.

How does this emotionally engage us? Because, on reflection, we see that the comma has probably had more impact on human lives than all the military leaders in history. Their exploits come and go, but the revolution wrought by the comma's power will outlive them all.

Identifying Heroic Qualities

Main heroic quality:

Elegant ingeniousness

Alternative(s):

Influence in transforming human societies

Images that capture the heroic quality:

The tiny comma resting in one side of a scale and all the military forces with their armor, tanks, and guns on the other, and the comma dragging the scale down and driving the other upwards. The slight mark on paper making language, which had always been an oral exchange from mouth to ear, hospitable to the eye. Language has become silent, reading has become accessible to all, and the lowly comma has helped create a revolution in building democracy by giving this new power to access text to all.

2. Organizing the Topic Into a Narrative Structure

Initial Access

What aspect of the topic best embodies the heroic qualities identified as central to the topic?

Does this expose some extreme of experience or limit of reality?

What image can help capture this aspect?

A newspaper editor might ask, "What's the story here?" Our story is the revolution that has had an immense impact on our civilization and even on our very sense of ourselves. It is the story of the profound shift from the reliance on the ear for access to knowledge to reliance on the eye. It is a part of the story we have briefly examined, of the West moving in from an oral to an oral and literate culture, with all that that has entailed. In this story, the comma plays a decisive role in transforming text so that it can be easily read and its meaning easily grasped. It is an important part, also, of the story of democracy, as reading texts became increasingly less a task for a skilled elite and more accessible to all. Spaces between words, paragraphs, subheadings, capitals and lower-case letters, periods or full stops, quotation marks, exclamation points, and the mighty comma all help to divide up the text into meaning chunks that elegantly permit us to engage in this curious, silent communication.

Given our narrative line, we may decide to take the punctuation marks either in the sequence of their historical development or in the degree of their impact on making the page hospitable to the eye, which turns out to be much the same. This narrative line, incidentally, brings some items into the topic not normally considered matters of punctuation, such as the separation of words by spaces. (The first punctuation mark was the ancient Roman invention of inserting a period between words to separate them. It was called an *interpunctum*, a dot half-way up the line of letters, not at the base of the line where we place it today.)

Ms. Lopez began with just that, seeing what a dramatic impact spaces have on students' ability to read or at least begin to sort out the page of text. She prepared a series of sheets of the same text but each page was changed by a punctuation invention. The first sheet was the text as it might have appeared in the earliest form of writing. The next sheet showed the effect of the invention of capitals and lower-case letters, the next the mighty comma and full stop, and so on. Each item was introduced in terms of its contribution to the move from ear to eye, and each was presented in terms of the simple elegance and ingenuity by which it achieved its dramatic impact. Here are just three of the sheets she used:

Sheet 1

THEFIRSTACTIVITYOFTHECLASSMIGHTINVOLVEGIVING
THESTUDENTSAPIECEOFTEXTWITHOUTANYPUNCTUATION
SIMPLYALLTHEWORDSFLOWINGTOGETHERWITHNOBREAKS
COMMASPERIODSORANYOTHEROFTHEELEGANTAND
ECONOMICALCUESTHATMAKETEXTSEASILYACCESSIBLETO
THEEYEHEYWHATDOYOUMAKEOFTHISTHETEACHERCOULD
ASKJUSTSEEINGHOWMUCHMOREDIFFICULTITISTOREADWILL
GIVESOMEIMMEDIATESENSEOFAVALUEOFPUNCTUATION
HAVETHESTUDENTSREADTHETEXTALOUDTOHEARRATHER
THANSEEHOWMUCHEASIERITISTOTHENMAKESENSEOF
CHOOSESOMETHINGWITHLOTSOFQUOTATIONSSUBHEADINGS
ANDSOONGRAPHICILLISTRATIONEHWHATSALLTHATSOME
STUDENTMIGHTSAY

Sheet 2

THE FIRST ACTIVITY OF THE CLASS MIGHT INVOLVE GIVING THE STUDENTS A PIECE OF TEXT WITHOUT ANY PUNCTUATION SIMPLY ALL THE WORDS FLOWING TOGETHER WITH NO BREAKS COMMAS FULL STOPS OR ANY OTHER OF THE ELEGANT AND ECONOMICAL CUES THAT MAKE TEXTS EASILY ACCESSIBLE TO THE EYE HEY WHAT DO YOU MAKE OF THIS THE TEACHER COULD ASK JUST SEEING HOW MUCH MORE DIFFICULT IT IS TO READ WILL GIVE SOME IMMEDIATE SENSE OF A VALUE OF PUNCTUATION HAVE THE STUDENTS READ THE TEXT ALOUD TO HEAR RATHER THAN SEE HOW MUCH EASIER IT IS TO THEN MAKE SENSE OF CHOOSE SOMETHING WITH LOTS OF QUOTATIONS SUBHEADINGS AND SO ON GRAPHIC ILLISTRATION EH WHATS ALL THAT SOME STUDENT MIGHT SAY

Sheet 3

The first activity of the class might involve giving the students a piece of text without any punctuation, simply all the words flowing together with no breaks, commas, full stops, or any other of the elegant and economical cues that make texts easily accessible to the eye.

"Hey, what do you make of this?" the teacher could ask.

Just seeing how much more difficult it is to read will give some immediate sense of a value of punctuation. Have the students read the text aloud to hear rather than see how much easier it is to then make sense of. Choose something with lots of quotations, subheadings, and so on.

Graphic illustration, eh?

"What's all that?" some student might say.

Depending on the students, the teacher might prepare additional sheets. For the less advanced students, Ms. Lopez composed a quite simple piece of capitalized, spaceless writing; for more advanced students, she prepared a longer and more complex piece. Students were invited to begin by putting a line where they thought there should be a division between words. After that they were invited to locate where the commas or periods should go. And so on. Even students with very little skill in reading began identifying word groupings. For students who might have difficulty even with this task, one could unscramble the words used in the text on a separate sheet.

Images that capture heroic quality:

The comma as superhero

Exotic or extreme content that best embodies the heroic quality:

The unsuspected power of the comma—along with its tiny allies: the period, spaces, quotation marks, and so on—as transformer of the world

Humanizing the Content

What aspects of the story best illustrate the human emotions in it and evoke a sense of wonder?

What ideals or challenges (or both) to tradition or convention are evident in the content?

We can humanize the material by reference to the hopes of those who introduced the various innovations. We can see the struggles that they were involved in and the interests of those who resisted the innovations. Ms. Lopez was able to draw on some of the background materials made available by the Imaginative Education Research Group. So she was able to talk and show illustrations about the particular effects of each innovation, demonstrating the heroic quality of the tiny punctuation allies, led by the comma. It wasn't necessary to locate individual people; the comma itself was imbued with the heroic qualities that made it engaging to the students' imaginations.

Our research was able to add anecdotes about some of the particular heroes of this story. Useful resources included Ivan Illich's (1993) book on Hugh of St. Victor and the rich set of examples in David Olson's (1994) *The World on Paper*. Ms. Lopez used the examples to show how huge social and psychological changes were brought about by making texts easily readable. The truly revolutionary nature of punctuation was emphasized early on. Its inventors transformed the world and people's lives much more than Caesar or Napoleon did or all the celebrated military and political figures who loom large in our history books. But the comma was invented by someone, and Ms. Lopez dramatized the image of a medieval monk, courteously working in his cell to make his manuscript page more easy to read and coming up with this tiny mark that indeed helped to make reading a much easier activity for all.

She also demonstrated to the students the general principle of comma use that refers back to their own body as its human core. They were encouraged to think of writing as making oral language visible. Where we pause when speaking, we use punctuation marks when writing; the comma serves for brief pauses and the period for longer pauses. She suggested this as the most general fall-back rule when they were uncertain, making clear that it was not itself a sure guide.

> **What content can be best shown in terms of hopes, fears, intentions or other emotions?**
>
> The comma and its allies being invented as a result of courtesy, as the medieval monk struggles to make his manuscript easier to read, thereby leading to a revolution that has transformed the world.

Pursuing Details

What parts of the topic can the students best explore in exhaustive detail?

One aspect of comma use students might study in exhaustive detail is how different meanings can be created by strategic placement of commas within the same sentence or phrase. Ms. Lopez made a lot of use of sets of unpunctuated sentences, asking the students to try to create different meanings by changing only the comma use. Here are some of the simplest she used:

- "You have no idea what I think" can also become the different "You have no idea what, I think."
- "A pretty tall girl" can be "A pretty, tall girl" or "A pretty tall girl"—as in a rather tall girl.
- "Birds that migrate occasionally fly high" yields "Birds that migrate occasionally, fly high" and "Birds that migrate, occasionally fly high."
- "The year before John went away" could be changed by a comma to the different meaning "The year before, John went away."
- "Jane claimed John made the mess" is crucially different from "Jane, claimed John, made the mess."

The students were then told about the overly dramatic but rather careless actor performing in Macbeth who was supposed to say "Go, get him surgeons," but being careless about commas, instead shouted "Go get him, surgeons." A more well-known one is "A woman, without her man, is nothing," is dramatically changed to "A woman: without her, man is nothing."

Students were also given simple introductory materials with which to study the history of the comma and then were encouraged to conduct an Internet search to add to their knowledge. The students were given basic information, such as that the word came directly from the Greek *komma* for "clause" or "segment;" the various ways commas have been indicated, as with a "/" slash mark in early medieval times; and how important the emperor Charlemagne was in initially establishing our current use of the comma.

Ms. Lopez divided the class into twos and threes and gave one group the task of summarizing the arguments in favor of including and omitting the final comma in a series. Some argued for "a, b, and c," whereas others defended "a, b and c" (reflecting a difference between American and British usage. She had discussed the pros and cons before giving the students the task of summarizing.) Other students were given other rules to explore and report back on. One clear result of this activity was to demonstrate that there are no ultimate rules for comma use and that people's uses through history and today vary. The main rule might be understood to be the courtesy that produces clarity for the eye of the reader.

> **List those aspects of the topic that students can explore exhaustively:**
>
> The variety of ways a comma can be used to change a sentence; the history of the comma; the various and variable rules of comma use

3. CONCLUSION

How can we best bring the topic to satisfactory closure?

How can the student feel this satisfaction?

Ms. Lopez gave students pieces of unpunctuated text and asked them to transform the meaning by their uses of punctuation—a more elaborate form of the exercise mentioned earlier. A nice example used to introduce this exercise was taken from Donald J. Sobol's (1986) *Encyclopedia Brown* stories:

Tyrone wants to send his girlfriend a message that he wrote as,

How I long for a girl who understands what true romance is all about. You are sweet and faithful. Girls who are unlike you kiss the first boy who comes along, Adorabelle. I'd like to praise your beauty forever. I can't stop thinking you are the prettiest girl alive. Thine, Tyrone.

Unfortunately, Tyrone read the message to Adorabelle's sister over the phone. She wrote it down, but had no idea how to punctuate it in a way that would capture Tyrone's meaning. Poor Adorabelle received this message:

How I long for a girl who understands what true romance is. All about you are sweet and faithful girls who are unlike you. Kiss the first boy who comes along, Adorabelle. I'd like to praise your beauty forever. I can't. Stop thinking you are the prettiest girl alive. Thine, Tyrone.

The students clearly enjoyed repunctuating a piece of text to make it mean something dramatically different. Ms. Lopez prepared a number of unpunctuated sentences to which commas could be added so that different meanings would be imposed on the words. (She used the examples just given and those from the previous chapter: "Private! No swimming allowed!" means something quite different when punctuated as "Private? No. Swimming allowed." Similarly, "I'm sorry you can't come with us," means something different from "I'm sorry. You can't come with us." Or "The butler stood at the door and called the guests' names" is radically changed, by a tiny difference of punctuation, to "The butler stood at the door and called the guests names.")

She had some examples of eighteenth-century writers in English who favored the dash over commas and periods so that students might conclude the unit by considering the arbitrariness of our forms of punctuation. For the final exercise, students were given a few lines of unpunctuated text to work with and asked to invent at least one new punctuation mark in the process, displacing one of the current conventions if they wished. The emphasis was on acknowledging the simple elegance and ingenuity of our techniques of punctuation but recognizing that they are only conventions, useful as long as they are useful, to be changed and discarded when they might be improved on. But their uses and values became clear as students dealt with texts that lacked them. The exercises were successful in meeting their purpose of helping to bring out the inventiveness involved in punctuation and giving students some sense of wonder about its impact.

Concluding activities:

Playing with punctuation to influence meaning to add to the growing understanding of the power of the comma and its small allies

4. EVALUATION

How can we know that the content has been learned and understood and has engaged and stimulated students' imaginations?

Any of the traditional forms of evaluation can be used, but in addition, teachers might want to get some measure of how far students' imaginations have been engaged by the topic. In addition, the concluding activities are also evaluative in nature.

Ms. Lopez added careful observation of the degree to which individual students recognized that punctuation is not merely a utilitarian convention but is a product of much ingenuity to traditional evaluative techniques. Those taken-for-granted squiggles and marks on a page have a heroic quality of their own as elegant and ingenious revolutionaries in a great adventure. We were not able to find a means of getting any objective index of students' sense of the heroic quality of the comma but if the teacher is sensitive to its importance, some alertness to it can lead at least to an informal qualitative assessment.

Some of the exercises in the main body of the lesson, such as having the students punctuate the same sentence in two ways in order to produce different meanings, were also used to yield good evaluative data.

Forms of evaluation to be used:

Recall of general rules, as exemplified in students being able to use them on set texts; observation of students' sense of the heroic nature of the comma in human history; exercises in which students show their understanding of how different uses of the comma in the same text can produce different meanings

The Frameworks and You

The frameworks presented are offered as tools that I hope you find useful. When adapted for particular units, they can stimulate your imagination and thereby lead to lessons that stimulate students' imaginations, too.

But what about the time involved in designing these kinds of lessons? What about the regular teachers hacking away in the trenches, with barely enough time to plan and certainly not enough time to retool all the materials and lesson plans they currently have? It may be that their current approach, materials, and plans do the job well enough and sometimes very well indeed. Why take on something like the planning frameworks outlined in this chapter?

Many teachers have found that this approach gives them a new planning technique and also a new approach to their work that energizes them, making their teaching more engaging for their students and for themselves. Also, while seeing this for the first time might make it seem a rather contrived approach to planning, our experience has been that many teachers find that they come to think in the form of the planning frameworks quite quickly. It seems a more natural way of planning than the old objectives techniques to many. Also, many teachers simply take a few of the features of the frameworks and incorporate them into their usual procedures.

Conclusion

When I began writing this book, I had the joy of playing daily with our first grandchild. At one year, he has what we can distinguish as a vocabulary of three distinct sounds. First, a loud "a," as in "at," is his sound for the cat. The "a" is clearly derived from our use of *cat*, with a slight modulation which seems to be his acknowledgement of the sound the cat makes—usually meowing in terror as the eager infant crawls energetically towards her shouting "a," "a," "a." Second, an "eh" sound, spoken with some urgency or irritation, seems to mean "again." It is used when one has finished spinning his wooden top or when he has knocked down some plastic containers that he wants erected so he can knock them down again. There is also a sound somewhere between the other two that designates people and which commonly greets me in the morning.

During the next two years, if he follows the developmental pattern common to nearly all humans, language will begin to become more differentiated and elaborate, and then it will develop in a burst that is always a little like a miracle. Whether one accepts Stephen Pinker's claim that we have a "language instinct" (Pinker, 1994), we are certainly supremely sensitive to language, and it emerges in our development with great reliability. We are genetically predisposed to become oral language users.

We are not genetically predisposed to become literate. The learning that is necessary to become efficiently literate seems different in some significant ways from that which leads to our development of oral language. Indeed, we are inclined to say that orality develops, whereas literacy is learned. The most informed guesses today suggest that oral language developed around two hundred thousand years ago. Literacy is a relatively recently invented trick, whose great utility has persuaded everyone who can to learn and exploit its great uses. Our grandson will likely not become literate with the thoughtless ease with which he is beginning to become an oral language user.

What we hope to witness over the next couple of years in our grandson's experience is a kind of vastly accelerated recapitulation of a process his long-distant ancestors went through in developing language in the first place.

The initial effortless articulation of grandchildren and the so often hard, hard work of acquiring literacy seem worlds apart. One is supported by our evolutionary development; the other is a technical invention of a few thousand years ago. The latter, however, is complicatedly tied to the former. I think that by exposing the cognitive tools underlying our uses of language, some of the ties are also exposed. As a consequence we can devise better ways of helping children as well as adults with the hard work of taking into themselves that technical invention and enjoying the vast range of what it can do for us.

Supplementary Material

Further examples of varied uses of the imaginative approach to teaching can be found on the Web site of the Imaginative Education Research group at www.ierg.net. There you will find many more examples in a wide variety of curriculum areas. There are text, audio, and video supports that you may download for free.

Appendix

Responses to the "Teachers, Try It Out" Questions

Gillian C. Judson

Chapter 1. Using the Story Form: Meeting Objectives by Engaging Feelings

1. You are introducing suffixes that indicate past tense. How can you fit this task into a story form?

Here's a story using verbs that take an "ed" in the past tense. Introduce the students to Mr. Beentheredonethat, known to his friends as "Ed." Ed is a clingy man. He is not a leader but a follower who really changes those he hooks onto. Ed is very influential. When Ed hangs out with his active buddies, *walk, laugh,* or *play,* for example, he makes them old news. Students could then identify more of Ed's "buddies" that he can, and does, make "old news" (ski, jump, look . . .).

The lesson (and story) could be expanded to say that Ed doesn't like to be outdone by any other "e," so if there is already an "e" at the end of the word he wants to-be attached to, he bumps it off and takes over (e.g., hike: hiked).

2. You want to draw students' attention to detailed word forms, so you decide to design a class on recognizing words within words (e.g., "at" in "cat" or "ate" in "plate"). How can you fit this task into a story form?

    a. Draw students' attention to word forms containing the word *ear* by having a game of hide and seek, first with the ear and then the eye. Read the students a short text and ask where *ear* is hiding. Then have the students read the text and identify where *ear* is hiding. Here is a possible text:

Once upon a time there was a b*ear* named Bob who was absolutely f*ear*less. No f*ear* at all. This d*ear* b*ear* skateboarded in competitions every y*ear* that were n*ear* his home and also cl*ear* across the country. Did you h*ear* what happened to him last y*ear*? He took a fall that caused him to shed a t*ear*. Thankfully he had on all his g*ear*. So now we know Bob has one f*ear*: falling on his r*ear*.

Students could be encouraged to make up their own hide-and-seek stories with other detailed words (*ink*—stink, link, pink, rink, fink, wink . . .)

b. Tell students about a "chameleon" word, such as *in* (or *at* or *up*). Describe the chameleon using words that contain it and then have students expand the search looking for the word disguised within other words. The following could be an introduction to the chameleon *in*:

"I th*in*k *in* has th*in* sk*in* but perhaps just on the sh*in* or f*in*. *In* likes to w*in* P*in* the Tail on the Donkey. Where else is *in* hiding?"

Or *at*:

"I'll st*at*e for the record that *at* is sometimes disguised as a f*at* r*at*. He s*at* under the doorm*at* the last time I saw him."

3. You want to draw students' attention to differences between written and oral forms of language. How can you fit this task into a story form?

a. The teacher could use Ear and Eye as characters in a story that highlights the difference between oral and written forms of language. Ear and Eye can be two friends that live in the same hometown of Head. When asked to remember things, they go about the task very differently: Ear likes to hear, and Eye likes to spy. Ear thinks about what he has to remember in the form of a narrative, creating visual images and making up rhymes and patterns to help him. Eye on the other hand takes the information to be learned, converts it into symbolic code and then organizes the code into words. The words created form tables, charts, and lists.

b. The class could brainstorm the best ways to remember things without writing them down (narrative, imagery, rhyme, rhythm and pattern, metaphor, etc.). These are elements of oral language. Students could then be asked to remember these different elements of oral language by using one or more of the strategies. For example, they could create a vivid mental image that would contain the different strategies of oral language in action or form a story that reflects oral ways of understanding. For the written language equivalent, students would need to employ lists, charts, tables, and so on, to memorize the strategies and ways of understanding that characterize written language.

Chapter 2. Images We Care About: Too, Two, and To

1. Compose a story about homophones—like *to*, *two*, and *too*—that brings out their distinct meanings through creation of personalities that are a reflection of the separate words and their meanings.

by, buy, bye: Mr. *By* is always huddled up to someone; he loves to cuddle. Because he lives on a slant, he can be near others quite easily. Mr. *Buy* has no time to cuddle. He is too busy shopping. That bag of his (the 'u') needs to be filled with beautiful merchandise. *Bye* (often accompanied by his twin brother, *Bye*) cannot settle in one place. He is on the move and never stays put for too long.

do, due, dew: That Ms. *Do*, she is all about action. She always encourages her friends to do what they want and is known for her optimism. Then there is Ms. *Due* who, sadly, is in trouble with the bank; there are collectors after her requesting money: "Fill up the sack (the 'u') with what you owe us!" they all say. Finally, Ms. *Dew* is definitely a morning person. Up with the dawn, she stays out of sight in the afternoon and evening. She is particularly fond of grass tips ('w'); she loves to lie around there. She isn't all that exciting, however, and has been called a bit of a drip.

so, sew, sow: *So* is a lonely little creature. Although well-balanced in character, this one always needs back-up. *So* what? *So* always needs somebody else to help him out. *So* is nothing but unfinished business. *So* has a cousin named *Sew* who loves to make things! She is particularly fond of fabrics and requires a steady hand and good eyesight to do her work. She is really funny—she had me in stitches (ha ha)! The eye of a needle ('e') is central to her very being. And then there is *Sow*. Sow loves the spring. He tends to be messy, though, and hangs out in the dirt a lot. *Sow*, to be honest, is a bit "seedy" and doesn't live in the best part of town.

meet, meat: Have I introduced you to *Meet*? She is a very social person who shrieks with joy when she runs into old friends. *Meet* has a cousin who looks a lot like her but is actually very different gravy. Meet's cousin's name is *Meat*. *Meat* is just too busy eating to socialize. You'll find him at most BBQs—he's a really big fan of the grill.

no, know: I have never met such an abrupt, short, *negative* character as that *No* person. So unwilling to try new things! So negative! I would much rather spend time with *Know*: I feel so smart when I'm with her. She likes to be aware of what is going on here and *now*. In order to be in her group of friends (to be in the *know*), you have to be aware of what is going on in the world.

toe, tow: Let me introduce you to *Toe*. Toe is rarely alone. She shares a place with four siblings, and they are a huge support to each other. Toe kind of looks like her "e" puts a nail on. And then there is *Tow*, a really strong guy. He pulls people around who can't move on their own. Just look how Tow's "w" can hook those folks on!

2. How can images help you and your students explore compound words, particularly how they sometimes reflect the meaning of the distinct words put together (e.g., "bedroom") and sometimes produce somewhat new meanings (e.g., "footlocker").

Caregiver: My grandma is the kindest, most caring and giving person I know. She looks after the whole family, including our pet frog, iguana, and tarantula. She loves us all very much and is constantly showing how much she loves and cares about us. One day my grandma wasn't feeling well, and I wanted to care for her for a change. So I did. I did all the chores around the house. *I* was the caregiver until she felt better.

Sweetheart: John jumped down the school steps in front of Mary, slipped on an apple core, and really twisted his ankle. He stood up, and it really hurt. "Oh shoot, now I can't do my paper round! What'll I do?" "I'll do it for you," Mary said. John didn't want to let her, even though she had walked the round with him a few times, because they were good friends and really liked each other. It was a hot day, and Mary spent two hours delivering the papers, finally coming back, tired and thirsty, to John's house. As she went into the house, she smelled something delicious. He shouted for her to come into the kitchen, and there on the counter was a tall glass of milk, and he had made a heart-shaped cookie with colored sprinkles all over it. "It's a sweet heart for my sweetheart," he smiled.

Workhorse: Jenny lives on a farm with her mom, dad, brother, three chickens, and horse. Her dad was up early one morning attaching a plow to the back of the horse. "Why are you doing that, daddy?" "Our tractor is not working, and I need to plow the field in order to plant the seeds. Henry can do the work of the tractor by pulling the plow." Later that day Jenny was feeling tired because she had been doing homework all day. Her brother asked her to do his chores for him because he wasn't feeling well. She probably should have helped her brother but felt angry and tired instead and said to him, "No way! I'm not your workhorse! Ask Henry to do it for you!"

3. How can you encourage writing activities by building on emotionally charged images?

How Are You Today? In this activity students learn adjectives associated with different emotions. To begin, students could be asked to imagine what their face looks like up close in a mirror. (Students could actually stare into mirrors for this activity.) They can be told to focus closely on their eyes, eyebrows, nose, dimples, mouth, wrinkles, so on. What does "happy" look like? What does "sad" look like? "surprised"? "tired"? Students can then draw these faces and write the appropriate adjective next to them. They can then be asked to imagine what makes them feel these emotions—happy, surprised, worried, and so on—in order to imagine the circumstances or triggers for them. They can identify key words from these images and could build upon these images and emotions, expanding their adjective lists to include more sophisticated language.

What's in a Season? In this activity students use images to develop vocabulary around different activities and seasons. Ask students what their favorite outdoor activity is. Encourage them to imagine as vividly as possible what they look like and what their surrounding environment looks like as they do this activity. Have them identify key words from the image and write down features of the season (whether adjectives or words associated with the environment, climate, or even themselves). Ask students to imagine doing the same activity in a different season. How does the activity change? What happens to the image? More key words may be identified. How does this different season (climate, weather conditions, etc.) influence the clothing worn or the activity itself? (e.g., would you ski in summer?). The aim would be to develop vocabulary around students' favorite activities (adverbs, nouns, and adjectives) as well as around climate and weather.

No Walk in the Park: In this activity the teacher helps the students create a mental image in their minds of a peaceful walk in the park. The teacher incorporates a variety of different animals in the image, however, and students are to respond to the appearance of each animal in unique ways. Students are asked to employ different adjectives to describe the animals as well as different verbs and adverbs to describe their actions. The image-provoking text could be something like this:

> It is a beautiful spring morning in (wherever). The sun shines brightly in the sky, leaving a pattern of light across the path as you stroll through the forest. A slight breeze blows, filling your lungs with sweet spring air. Suddenly, emerging from the bushes and landing directly in front of you, there is a (fox, giraffe, slug, hamster, grizzly bear, etc.). The animal is (adjectives). You feel (adjective) and you immediately (verb, adverb).

What's Your Favorite Color? In this activity students explore nouns, adjectives, and use of the superlative. They begin by identifying their favorite color. Next they will be asked how many different shades there are of their favorite color. What objects in the world are that color? These words may be written down. What object best represents that color? (So what is the bluest, the reddest, etc.?) Ask them to imagine being completely surrounded by these objects, completely surrounded by this color. What words describe this image? Alternatively, all students can be asked to think of a color that the teacher selects, such as red or yellow or whatever, and follow the same steps. The next activity could be with an opposite color: adjectives could be compared and contrasted, listed, and so forth.

Chapter 3. Binary Opposites: Goldilocks and Civil War

1. How might you exploit students' engagement by oppositions and mediation by using a large sheet of paper stuck on a wall of the classroom? What kinds of activities would you invite them to perform?

    a. With two large sheets of paper attached to opposite sides of the classroom, teachers could have the students write opposite words on opposite sides of the classroom in ways that describe their meaning. For example,

small   **large**

dark   light

wide   narrow

b. The class could also collect oxymorons, adding them each week throughout the year to a large sheet of paper attached to the wall. Students could have fun role-playing situations in which the oxymorons would be used and that express their meaning. Students may also create their own oxymorons illustrating their meaning in a skit or short, written narrative.

c. The teacher could briefly recount how he or she arrived at school that day in as descriptive a way as possible, inviting students to write down the opposites to what they hear on sheets of paper as they listen to the story. Students could work in teams to write down as many corresponding opposites as possible. The "new" text that results is likely to be quite humorous. An example of a possible descriptive text follows:

> This beautiful (ugly) morning (evening) as I arrived at (left) school, I noticed a tiny (huge) white (black) snowflake falling from (to) the sky (ground). I was completely (incompletely) thrilled (devastated) because today (yesterday, tomorrow?) is (was) my birthday, and I love (hate) snow.

2. How might you ask students to tell a story from their own experience in a way that builds on opposites and mediation?

a. Teachers could invite students to think of their *most* embarrassing moment. Students could identify the language in their story that brings out the extreme embarrassment they associate with the event. They could then be asked to change the event by providing opposites to details in the story, especially those details that make the event embarrassing. Students could then discuss to what degree different language—opposites in this case—increase or decrease the degree of embarrassment they associate with the event.

b. Most students are quick to say that their life is a bit boring and that nothing ever happens. The teacher could develop vocabulary around oppositions and mediation by having students describe a typical Saturday in a few sentences (oral first and then written). Students could then be encouraged to use vocabulary that makes the day much more dramatic: they would exaggerate a typical day. To add texture and force to their boring experiences, they could then reverse the exaggerations in the other direction, using opposites where possible. Boring is in the "eye" of the beholder!

3. After students have read or listened to many stories in a particular genre (fairy stories, family tales, monster stories), how could you use oppositions and mediation to explore those stories and that genre more fully?

a. Teachers could ask students to take several stories from their favorite genres and identify the oppositions contained within these stories. They could then write an announcement based on these oppositions that might appear in a local paper, introducing the movie form of the book.

b. Students could take the oppositions that characterize their favorite genre (e.g., a monster story) and use these to write their own story of a *different* genre (e.g., a family tale). The results could be quite unique! Afterwards they could decide what makes a story suitable for different audiences and age groups. Moreover, they could discuss what they consider to be the necessary ingredients for each genre and write a How-To book (another genre) for different styles of story.

Chapter 4. Literal and Metaphoric Talk: "Like a Spring-Woken Tree"

1. How might you use metaphors to help the students see the classroom differently?

a. The teacher could ask the students to play a game of "Where Am I?" The teacher would describe different contexts in the magical land of Metaphor, and students would guess where that was. The "metaphorical" names of objects common to that environment would need to be prepared in advance. For example, in the "classroom" the teacher may say someone "sneakers" into the "thinking den" picks up the "ink river" and "scans the room" to "eyeball" which "knowledge seekers" have "flip-flopped" in and are at their "work stations" and so on.

b. Teachers could hold a Metaphor Hour. The students could participate in a Show and Tell activity in which they would bring something from home and describe it to the class metaphorically; they would not be permitted to use ordinary descriptors. Only after they had described the object could they show the class: hence, Show and Tell. This would be a fun activity after students had some experience working with metaphor.

2. One of the funnier uses of language occurs when people mix metaphors in a sentence, jumping from one metaphor to another wholly inconsistent one. For example, "He stepped up to the plate and grabbed the bull by the horn." A metaphor derived from baseball becomes confused with something a cowboy might do. "That wet blanket is a loose cannon," "Strike while the iron is in the fire," or (said by a school administrator whose budget was slashed) "Now we can just kiss that program right down the drain." What activity could you design so that students could consciously construct mixed metaphors and have some fun in the process?

a. The teacher could have students play the Telephone game, an activity in which broken lines of communication can result in bizarre messages. The teacher would tell each student in secret an object or situation they were to describe metaphorically. Because each person would be talking about a different object or situation, a humorous and incongruous combination of images would result.

b. In small groups, students could role-play different scenarios in which they would use language specific to the context (e.g., a baseball game [home run, striking out, etc.], birthday party [blowing out the candles, opening the presents, playing games], auction [sold to the man in the white coat!]). They would select three to five expressions that are most typical of the scenario. They would then combine their small groups to create short skits in which the messages would be combined to create bizarre expressions: "I blew out my candles and totally struck out!" "Going once, going twice, home run!" Acting out these expressions could be great fun.

3. How might you help students explore the commonest forms of language they hear—on TV, via MP3s, in their own interactions—by focusing on metaphor?

    a. Students could be asked to listen to some music or watch television in order to find examples of metaphors used in popular language. They would bring in their examples for a Show and Tell activity in which they describe the context in which the metaphor has been employed. Alternatively they could share the metaphor and have students guess in what context it was used. Students should also highlight how the term is or could be misunderstood. For example, something is "the bomb" if it is excellent. So if a student says something they did for homework was "the bomb," they mean it was a great job. This could easily be misunderstood, based on another metaphor— "bombing" something: "I bombed that test!" which means one did poorly.

    b. Students could bring in their favorite CD, book, or magazine in order to do a metaphor hunt and analysis. They could share their findings with the class through art, poetry, song, or dance. The possibilities are endless!

Chapter 5. Jokes: Drawing the Drapes

1. How could you use jokes or humor to encourage students to recognize that good reading habits involve predicting later sections of the text on the basis of what they have already read?

    a. Teachers could have students predict what will happen to certain characters based on what they already know of their different personalities using Knock-Knock or other types of basic jokes. Focusing on what is incongruous in the story or in the nature of the characters may assist students in making predictive jokes based on these qualities. Here are some jokes based on *Goldilocks and the Three Bears*:

> What did Goldilocks find when she
>   went into the house in the woods?
> The bare necessities! (groan)

> Why did Goldilocks run out of the house so quickly?
> She couldn't bare it any longer! (double groan)

Knock knock
Who's there?
If Goldilocks.
If Goldilocks who?
If Goldilocks the door, then the bears won't get in!
(triple groan)

Students could also play with the sounds of words as a means to predict:

What did Sleeping Beauty say when she was waiting
   for her photos?
Someday my prints will come.

Jokes of the form, "What do you get when you cross an (x) and a (y)?" could also be used to draw out a prediction based on the nature of the characters students are familiar with.

b. Teachers can have students make up alliterative statements about characters using their names and qualities to predict what may happen in the story. For example, "Super Susy will soon see some sinister and sly students stealing secret sewing sessions with Sarah, Susy's sister."

2. How can you use jokes to help students with spelling?

a. Jokes and humor have the power to draw attention to the written word, to objectify it in such a way that different spelling patterns may be easier to recognize. Students could learn about homophones by making up jokes that highlight the different meanings of the words, such as *meat* and *meet*:

(Meat, Meet) What did the *hungry* person say to the cow? Nice to *eat* you . . . oops, I mean *meat* you.

(Red, Read) What is black and white and read all over? A newspaper!

Students could also create miscommunications using homophones. Consider the following example:

(At a wine and cheese event for body parts)

Eye: What do you do?

Ear: Hear.

Eye: Yes, here, what do you *do?*

Ear: I said hear. I hear here. And *you?*

Eye: Oh, I see.

Ear: Great, but what about *you?*

Eye: Here?

Ear: Yes, like me!

Eye: No. I see . . .

b. The teacher could draw attention to the spelling of words in general and to the meaning of the words through basic jokes:

What do you call a bear with no ear?
A "b"

3. Design a strategy for routinely using humor in teaching vocabulary expansion.

a. The teacher could have a daily Joke Time in which a different student each day has a chance to share a joke with the class. Joke books are filled with plays on words and can be useful tools for teachers. They are often based on themes that could parallel specific curriculum content—for example, jokes about animals, plants, or school. The jokes could be looked at in terms of why they are funny, and more jokes of that genre could be formulated by students.

b. Students could be asked to create quirky characters by employing alliteration; seeking words with the same sound would lead students to expand their vocabularies. For example, the teacher could write on the board: Meet _____ Mr. Meat. What adjective starting with "m" could students use to complete the sentence? Marvelous? Muscular? Medium-rare?

Chapter 6. Rhyme and Rhythm: Mickey Mouse's Underwear

1. Can you think of a technique, based on rhyme and rhythm, that might be used to teach spelling?

a. Students could study homophones and then create rhymes that indicate their different meanings. They could put the different rhymes into a "homophone rap." For example, "Eat your meat and meet on the street" or "If I go, too, with you makes two."

b. Students could think of some words they find difficult to spell and then think of a rhyme that would highlight the unique spelling. For example, take the word "climb": Climb a tree, end with *b*.

2. How could rhyme and rhythm be used to teach the use of full stops and commas?

a. Teachers can have students act out sentences with different body motions for periods, commas, and other punctuation marks. They may march on the spot while a sentence is read and then act out different forms of punctuation as they are required. The action for a period may be a little jump with arms by the sides and legs together. The action for a comma may be a droopy tilt of the body to either side, in a brief pause between other actions. The students could be encouraged to think of actions that best illustrate the function of the different punctuation marks.

b. A basic chant (with a snap-snap-clap pattern) would help students remember the rules for use of different punctuation marks. For example,

> A period is just a dot; it really doesn't take a lot;
> After a period start anew, use a Capital as a cue;
> With a period the phrase is done, try it out—have
> some fun!

This very cheesy rap took about three minutes to make up (you could probably tell). The same could be done by the teacher or by students themselves for other forms of punctuation.

3. How might rhyme and rhythm be used to teach students to identify the main point of a short text?

a. Students could read a text and identify the main themes contained within it. They could then shape those themes into a short poem based on a couplet format. They may also focus on the images the text evokes for them and select key words to describe these images. The key words could serve as a basis for a short, reflective poem about the text.

b. Students could learn to identify the main themes in a text based on the mental images that they see as they read. They could select key words from the images that would represent main ideas. With these they could create clapping or snapping patterns (however they wanted to create a beat) that would express that theme. Take "fear" for example. What does "fear" sound like? What sounds correspond with the image the text evokes? What does "joy" sound like? What is the rhythm of "joy"?

Chapter 8. Extremes:
The Queueing Subbookkeeper

1. Take three items from the *Guinness Book of World Records* (2002) and show how they could be used to construct engaging lessons in the use of capitalization and punctuation.

   a. Student could first be taught the different rules around capitalization (proper names of people, places, months and days, trademark names, countries, nationalities, words in a title, etc.). The teacher could then provide a short text to the students from the *Guinness Book of World Records* that has no capitalization, and students could rewrite it using capitals where appropriate. Teachers could select amazing facts and records that have any number of capitalization requirements (such as those containing the names of trademark products, places, etc.). Consider the following two examples in which all capital letters have been eliminated and students could be asked to provide the correct capitalization:

   i. "the loudest burp": "on april 5 2000 paul hunn (uk) registered a burp of 118.1 db—similar to being in the front row at a rock concert and only slightly quieter than the noise made by an airplane on a runway." (*Guinness Book of World Records*, p. 66, 2002)

   ii. "fastest pogo stick up the cn tower": ashrita furman (usa) pogo-sticked up the 1,899 steps of the cn tower, toronto, canada, in 57 min 51 seconds on july 23 1999—approximately one step every two seconds." (*Guinness Book of World Records*, 2002, p. 68)

   A follow-up activity could be to give titles to the loudest burper or best pogo-sticker. Students could discuss how the capital is then a mark of honor.

   b. Teachers may also take excerpts from the *Guinness Book of World Records* and leave off the title. Students could read the excerpts and come up with their own catchy titles using different forms of punctuation: question marks, exclamation marks, and so on.

Consider the possible titles students could create based on this excerpt about a rabbit with the longest ears or the world's biggest s'more:

> Toby III a black male English top bred by Phil Wheeler (U.K.) holds the record for the longest rabbit ears: they are an astounding 29.7 inches (75.6 cm) long and 7.18 inches (18.24 cm) wide. (*Guinness Book of World Records,* 2002, p. 102)

Possible titles: Show Me the Bunny! Did You Hear About the Hare? Listen Up, Every Bunny!

> The largest s'more, weighing 789 lb (357 kg), was created at the Cape Hatteras KOA Kampground in Rodanthe, North Carolina, on June 19, 1999. It contained 284 lb (128 kg) of Graham crackers, 374 lb (170 kg) of chocolate, and 131 lb (59 kg) of marshmallows. (in all, 10,000 marshmallows were roasted; *Guinness Book of World Records,* 2002, p. 120)

Possible titles: Gimme S'more! A Melted Marshmallow Monster! How Big Was the Campfire?

c. Teachers could also have students find some amazing facts of their own using textual or virtual sources that highlight wonderful limits, extremes of reality. The students would share the record-breaking information they have found by situating it in the context of the individual's (or thing's) life. The class could focus on how, using oral language, they could dramatize the information. Students could then write the same story using appropriate punctuation to illustrate the amazing fact. For example, students may begin with questions such as, "Do you know who the hairiest living human is? Do you know who has the biggest feet?" The exclamation mark would obviously be suitable for stating such exotic facts. Other forms of punctuation, such as the colon, semicolon, and apostrophe, could be explored in the same fashion by embedding them within a narrative based on these extreme examples. This activity would also draw out the differences between oral and written language and the ways in which different affective dimensions are expressed through written language.

2. Choose an obviously false story from a sensational paper—aliens landed, monster sighted—and design a lesson in critical reading.

a. It takes just one glance at a few headings from the *National Enquirer* to have suitable material for an activity in critical thinking. For example, two headlines in a sensationalist paper read, "Woman gives birth to horse" and "Aliens take over New York City." Students could first be asked to suspend disbelief and think about what kind of awesome event this would be if it were true. What image does this headline evoke for them? The class may discuss the implications of such an event:

- What would it mean for life as they know it?
- What would it mean for the future of humanity?

They could then identify what is ludicrous or incongruent about this supposed piece of news. A human giving birth to an animal such as a horse, for example, is biologically impossible. To further this activity, students could be asked to find what is amazing in the event should the ludicrous be removed. In this case, the notion of birth and reproduction would be a source of awe, wonder that could be examined. On the Internet students could look for extremes of the real event: the longest or largest baby ever born, the woman who gave birth to the largest number of children, the oldest woman to give birth, and so forth. This will reveal to students that the sensational exists in real world events as well as false events.

b. The foregoing example was based simply on headlines. A further activity would be for teachers to have students try to "report" this event before reading the actual article. Their narratives will be filled with fantastical elements of varying degrees. They could then read the article and identify how their own creations compare with the article. The activity should illustrate to students similarities in the two accounts: the one which they created completely independently of witnessing the event and the other supposedly based on "truth." What, the teacher may ask, does this indicate for *anything* we read? How can we read so that we do not accept everything as truth?

Chapter 9. Everyday Heroes:
Spiderman and the Comma

1. Plan a lesson or two in which students design a set of cards of their heroes to teach the proper and different uses of capital and lowercase letters, commas, and exclamation points, and how these might be used in a game the students might then play.

  a. Students could each do several cards for their heroes (like baseball or hockey cards with, for example, Einstein's picture on the front, with a brief caption, and appropriate information about the hero on the back). The teacher could make up a set of cards reflecting the different uses of the commas and exclamation points (this could be adapted to any form of punctuation or grammatical rule). This would involve writing the symbol (,) on one side and a rule of usage on the other side. For example, on the front you would write a giant '!' and on the back you would write one of the exclamation point's uses, such as "To end a sentence communicating an astonishing idea" or "To end a sentence when someone is yelling a command." If the game was to be played as a class, all of the students' hero cards would be in one pile and the punctuation cards in another. After splitting the class into two teams, one player from each team would select a card from each pile. The player would be required to use the information provided on the hero (or any knowledge they may have of that person) to give an example of the use outlined on the punctuation card. If the player did so correctly, the team would get a point.

  I have always found that students enjoy games where some sort of race is involved. To spice up the action in this game, a student from each team could be given the tasks and would have to run up to the board and write down the answer first in order to get a point. Alternatively, teachers could have a face off, where two students face each other, each selects a card, and, to get a point, one of the players has to create the sentence and be the first to say it aloud correctly.

  b. Another game based on the hero and comma or exclamation point cards described in the previous activity would require the class to form two teams. For each challenge (creating a sentence about a hero using the comma or exclamation point in the way described on the card, for example), students would need to use themselves to create the sentences. Each person would be a different word or punctuation mark in their sentence, which they would make by lining up. They would "become" their examples. This activity would promote teamwork and would require full-class participation.

2. Plan a lesson in outline form that uses students' associations with heroes to teach how to sort and prioritize information.

a. Teachers may ask students to identify someone they consider to be a hero. Next, students could list all of the qualities their hero demonstrates. What is the most important heroic quality of this person? They may prioritize the qualities and defend the order they have established. In pairs, students would share the quality they identified as most important. Each would defend the quality they selected and in so doing, argue for their hero. Looking next to the prioritized list each student has of heroic qualities, students would compare and contrast these lists. They may illustrate the similarities using a Venn diagram. Together they would identify the key features of a hero.

b. The teacher could select a few historical figures from various backgrounds for students to research. Students would conduct research in order to decide who they believe to be the most heroic. Once everyone has done the research and made their decisions, they would need to defend their choice. Students should write down the strengths and weaknesses of their chosen hero. They would be asked to identify the biggest weakness and the greatest strength. Students could debate based on these perceived strengths and weaknesses as to who is the truest hero. Following the debate, they would be encouraged to reevaluate whether they believed their person to be heroic.

3. How might you plan a lesson that encourages cooperation in editing and revising draft sentences, using text about students' heroes?

a. Students could be asked to write a brief biography-type description of their chosen heroes. They would then exchange their drafts with someone else in the class (preferably, someone who did not select the same individual). In proofreading each other's work, students would be asked to identify the language that portrays the individual as a hero. The proofreader would provide the writer with a list of strengths and weaknesses in the piece, as well as suggestions as to how to make it more convincing. Students could enact documentary-type (*Biography* style) presentations for the class as a concluding activity.

b. In pairs, students could cooperatively write, edit, and revise a children's book on a particular hero. They could also use their writing as a basis for a short poem or song about their hero. The focus of the activity would be on cooperation and collaboration throughout the process.

Chapter 10. Human Contexts: John Montagu, The Earl of Sandwich

1. How might you enrich the meaning of a short poem by setting it in the context of its author's life? Choose a poem and describe something of the author's life that would enable you to more richly teach about the poem.

Try situating the poetry of Shel Silverstein within the context of his life. Teachers might inspire children by telling them how Shel Silverstein began writing as a child. They can tell the children of *all* the talents he possessed, not simply the poetry and drawing he is often known for. Shel Silverstein was not only a cartoonist and a poet but also a composer, lyricist, and folksinger. The Irish Rovers sang and recorded his poem "The Unicorn Song." Sing this song with your students! Silverstein's writing contains something for everyone, and he hoped each person would discover something magical in his work. In reading his work, children and adults alike—dreamers, wishers, liars, pretenders, and more—are invited to imagine worlds unknown. *Where the Sidewalk Ends* offers a wealth of poems to use in your class, such as "Invitation" and "Magic."

2. How might you use the human quality of tenacity or of courage in teaching about some aspect of punctuation?

Exclamation Point: Teachers could introduce the class to the exemplary, highly outspoken, and rarely boring exclamation point. Exclamation has the power to create a sense of excitement and urgency in the reader! Exclamation can take a sentence that is seemingly ordinary and make it extraordinary! Exclamation adds force to the written word and helps to account for tone, volume, and intonation used in oral language to express excitement and other emotions. This sort of discussion is particularly suitable with increased communication using the Internet and e-mail. How do we express emotion through the written word beyond the words we choose? The teacher may illustrate this power to bring emotion into a text by discussing how simply sentences change with the presence of an exclamation point.

- "I won the lottery." versus "I won the lottery!"
- "Run quickly. The bear is coming." versus "Run quickly! The bear is coming!"

The class could discuss, moreover, why that particular symbol is used. Does it *look* powerful? Students could be asked to design a symbol they think would be more appropriate.

Question Mark: The question mark represents a frontier to the unknown. It can single-handedly transform something real into something unreal, something certain into something uncertain: for example, "We are going tonight." versus "We are going tonight?" Who knows for sure? The question mark opens up opportunities for knowing more about the world around us. Without asking questions, without evoking the power of the question mark, would we understand realms of sciences as we do? Would it be possible to research the world without using the question mark?

Apostrophe: The apostrophe is a presumptuous creature who, in conjunction with its sidekick "s" claims things for its owner. For example, it can claim coffee for Starbucks (Starbucks's coffee) or further, it can claim Starbucks's coffee for Betty (Betty's Starbucks's coffee). The apostrophe can even replace letters! When two words get together, as they often do when we use language casually, the new word may call upon the apostrophe for help. For example, "do" and "not" call upon the apostrophe to replace the second "o": don't. In some instances, this little hanging squiggle replaces two letters! What a lot of responsibility. For example, I will: I'll.

3. Design a lesson in which you would encourage students to recognize forms of language shaped by different strong emotions—love, anger, fear, and so on.

  a. Students could be asked how emotions are portrayed in oral versus written formats. They could demonstrate the differences between a love letter, and how love is portrayed or expressed in this format, versus a dialogue between two individuals in love. By highlighting the difficulties of expressing different strong emotions in written form, students would be introduced to the differences between oral and written forms of language and would explore the use of punctuation and writing style as a means to engage the reader.

  b. Students could have fun playing with the use of the imperative, orally and in written format. They could use the command form of language to express a variety of feelings by performing diverse emotions in different scenario skits. Choosing settings such as a circus, rodeo, stock market, casino, operating room, wedding, or police station, the teacher could have students express emotions that seem incongruous with the context.

Chapter 11. Collections and Hobbies: Alphabets and Beanie Babies

1. How might you design a classroom in such a way as to engage all the students in a game of spies and codes so that certain people can read the codes and others must attempt to decode them?

a. The teacher could divide the class into teams and assign each team a different area in the classroom as their territory. Each team would then create a secret code and write several phrases in it, displaying them clearly at the entrance to their terrain. To enter another team's territory, students would need to decode these access messages. Students could work individually or in pairs to see how many codes they could break in a certain amount of time. The teacher could even create an encoded message that students would need to solve before being granted "access" to recess.

b. The teacher could set up seven stations in the classroom that represent the seven continents on earth. Each continent would have a different encoded message that would need to be solved in order for the student to get a stamp on their "passport" and move elsewhere in their world journey. Students would be challenged to "travel" around the world as quickly as possible by decoding messages at each station. It would be wise for the teacher to connect the messages to something awesome or wonderful about the continents or their people.

2. What kind of collection would you recommend to help students not make mistakes in spelling commonly misspelled words?

Students could collect words that are spelled the same but are pronounced differently, depending on the context of the sentence: for example "I *read* everyday. I *read* that book last week." or "It is so *windy* outside! This is one *windy* road." The class could discuss the importance of contextual clues for comprehending the written word. It would be wise to draw on jokes and humor as well. Students could collect those jokes in which the humor is based on misunderstanding stemming from misspelling.

3. Can you think of a game that would involve students collecting punctuation marks and learning their proper use?

a. Teachers could begin by having students collect phrases in children's stories and popular magazines that contain examples of different uses of the six main forms of punctuation (. , : ; ! ').

Students could be encouraged to find phrases that contain the most uses of the same punctuation mark or the most different punctuation marks. Different point values could be assigned to the collected phrases. For example, a sentence that contains one punctuation mark (other than the period at the end) could have a value of 1. Sentences that contain two punctuation marks could be worth 2 points, three different punctuation marks, 3 points, and so forth. A sentence that contains four or even five different punctuation marks could be worth 10 points. Students could be challenged to find an improper use of punctuation for even more points (such as the improper use of an apostrophe for plural possessives). Finding an error in a text could even be an automatic win.

b. The first example is based on students seeking examples from texts of various kinds. In this game, students would be responsible for drawing on these collections as well as creating their own examples. The teacher would need at least two "punctuation" dice. It is easy to transform the sides of a regular die into a "punctuation" die by marking a different form of punctuation on each side; one would replace, for example, the "dots" indicating 1–6 with the following punctuation marks: . , : ; ! '. To play the game, the class could be divided into six small groups. Each group would be assigned a different punctuation mark as a team name (team comma, team period, etc.). The teacher would then roll the dice and students would be required to find in their collections of sentences (as discussed in the previous activity) examples of phrases with both forms of punctuation present. For example, if the teacher rolled a "," and a "!" students would need to find a phrase using these two forms. The first team to successfully find an example would win that round. To win an extra point, the team would have to come up with a new sentence that uses the same forms of punctuation.

A variation of the game could be for a team to win an automatic turn if their punctuation mark is rolled on both dice. So if the teacher rolled "snake eyes" with the colon marks (":" ":"), the colon team would have a chance to win double the points on a new roll of the dice. As the class advances in their use of the punctuation marks, the teacher could play with three or more "punctuation" dice.

Chapter 12. Graphic Organizers: Lists and Flowcharts

1. Give an example of how you might use a flowchart to clarify for students the main indicators of tenses and moods.

a. Begin by focusing on the structure of different tenses in terms of word combinations (auxiliary versus no auxiliary verbs). Provide students with examples which they would need to identify as a certain tense, using the flowchart. For example, the present tense can be expressed with one word (walk) or two words (am, is, are walking), the past tense can be expressed with one word (walked) or two words (was, were walking), and the future tense can be expressed with two words (will walk) or four words (am, is, are going to walk). The flow chart could start with having students find the subject and then decide if there is an auxiliary verb: how many words are there? Branching options could lead to the "ing" of either past or present or the "will" of the future tense. The "ing" option could further branch into looking at the tense of the auxiliary verb (Is it in the present: am, is, are? Or is it in the past: was, were?). The teacher could also do a flowchart focusing on different clue or key words within the sentence that would indicate different tenses (such as now, yesterday, tomorrow). Students could also construct their own flowcharts as a means to illustrate the structure of different verb tenses. The stages in the flowchart could reflect different ways to express a present, past or future tense.

b. Using a flowchart to clarify how moods are expressed could follow a discussion of different key words that reflect moods. Students could classify different adjectives and adverbs that indicate different emotions and then categorize these to build a flowchart that reflect different moods.

2. Design a rebus for some common expression or proverb.

    a. Man   (man over board)

      ———————

    Board

    b. hnaeyesdtlaeck   (needle in a haystack)

    c. investigation   THE POLICE   (to be under investigation
       to be   by the police)

3. How would you teach a lesson that focused on listing the names of vegetables, and how would you subdivide the lists?

    a. Make a list by asking the students to name all the different vegetables they have eaten in their lives. They may then add to the list, with the teacher's help, all those vegetables that they have heard of but never tried. Once the list is made, it can be divided into those eaten cooked or raw or both, those whose roots are eaten, those whose stems are eaten, those whose seeds are eaten, those whose leaves are eaten, those whose fruit is eaten, those whose heads are eaten, and perhaps those we don't eat at all—if there is such a vegetable.

    b. As a variation, the class itself could be the source of the list. First, all students' names would be written on the board. Next, the class would decide how the list could be subdivided (perhaps by gender, but why not by type of shoe: laces versus no laces?). These new lists could be further subdivided on the basis of hair color, hair length, foot size, eye color, number of letters in first name, number of buttons on clothing, and so on. The teacher could then introduce a fictional character to the class and the students would need to repeat their process to figure out where to place the new student.

    c. Students could explore careers by working with lists to categorize and subcategorize professions based on things like training required, skills, salary, risks involved, and so forth.

References

Ashton-Warner, S. (1972). *Spearpoint: Teacher in America*. New York: Knopf.

Bettelheim, B. (1976). *The uses of enchantment*. New York: Knopf.

Bruner, J. (1988). Discussion. *Yale Journal of Criticism, 2*(1), 28-37.

Callahan, R. (1962). *Education and the cult of efficiency*. Chicago: University of Chicago Press.

Egan, K. (1997). *The educated mind: How cognitive tools shape our understanding*. Chicago: University of Chicago Press.

Espy, W. R. (1982). *Have a word on me*. New York: Simon and Schuster.

Gardner, H., & Winner, E. (1979). The development of metaphoric competence: Implications for humanistic disciplines. In S. Sacks (Ed.), *On metaphor*, pp. 121-139. Chicago: University of Chicago Press.

Guinness Book of World Records. (2002). New York: Author.

Illich, I. (1993). *In the vineyard of the text: A commentary to Hugh's Didascalico*. Chicago: University of Chicago Press.

Imaginative Education Research Group. (2005). *A guide to imaginative education*. Burnaby, British Columbia, Canada: Simon Fraser University.

Lederer, R. (1989). *Crazy English*. New York: Pocket Books.

Luria, A. R. (1976). *Cognitive development: Its cultural and social foundations*. Cambridge, MA: Harvard University Press.

Olson, D. R. (1994). *The world on paper*. Cambridge, UK: Cambridge University Press.

Pinker, S. (1994). *The language instinct: How the mind creates language*. New York: Morrow.

Rieber, R. W., & Wollock, J. (Eds.). (1997). *The collected works of L. S. Vygotsky*. New York: Plenum.

Rorty, R. (1979). *Philosophy and the mirror of nature*. Princeton, NJ: Princeton University Press.

Sackville-West, V. (1930). *The king's daughter*. New York: Doubleday.

Sobol, D. J. (1986). *Encyclopedia Brown and the case of the mysterious handprints*. New York: Bantam Skylark.

Tanner, D., & Tanner, L. (1980). *Curriculum development: Theory into practice* (2nd ed.). New York: Macmillan.

Tyler, R. (1949). *Basic principles of curriculum and instruction*. Chicago: University of Chicago Press.

Vygotsky, L. (1962). *Thought and language* (E. Haufmann & G. Vakar, Trans.). Cambridge: MIT Press.

Vygotsky, L. (1978). *Mind in society: The development of higher psychological processes*. Cambridge, MA: Harvard University Press.

Index

**CORWIN
PRESS**

The Corwin Press logo—a raven striding across an open book—represents the union of courage and learning. Corwin Press is committed to improving education for all learners by publishing books and other professional development resources for those serving the field of PreK–12 education. By providing practical, hands-on materials, Corwin Press continues to carry out the promise of its motto: **"Helping Educators Do Their Work Better."**